SUCCESS SECRETS

Real-Life Stories to Inspire and Motivate

George Tan
BOOKSOUL International Pte Ltd, Singapore

BOOKSOUL inspire

World Scientific
NEW JERSEY • LONDON • SINGAPORE • BEIJING
SHANGHAI • HONG KONG • TAIPEI • CHENNAI

Published by

World Scientific Publishing Co. Pte. Ltd.

5 Toh Tuck Link, Singapore 596224

USA office: 27 Warren Street, Suite 401-402, Hackensack, NJ 07601

UK office: 57 Shelton Street, Covent Garden, London WC2H 9HE

British Library Cataloguing-in-Publication Data
A catalogue record for this book is available from the British Library.

SUCCESS SECRETS: REAL-LIFE STORIES TO INSPIRE AND MOTIVATE

ISBN-13 978-981-279-004-0 (pbk)
ISBN-10 981-279-004-7 (pbk)

Typeset by Stallion Press
Email: enquiries@stallionpress.com

Printed in Singapore by B & JO Enterprise

Success

I have learned that success is to be measured
not so much by the position that one has reached in life
as by the obstacles overcome while trying to succeed.

Booker T Washington
(1856–1915)

inspire

Dedicated to

mother

who wanted me to be successful

inspire

Dearest Mama,

Because of your. . .

Endurance	*I could bear unbearable hardship*
Self-reliance	*I did not fall into hopelessness*
Self-acceptance	*I appreciate my blessings and my troubles*
Resilience	*I am not defeated by setbacks*
Determination	*I developed a strong will to succeed*
Perseverance	*I never gave up hope*
Trustworthiness	*I value my integrity*
Love	*I conquered insurmountable obstacles*
Self-discipline	*I secured my future*
Humility	*I remember my roots*
Helpfulness	*I value friendship*
Backbone	*I am a man*
Steadfastness	*I could not bear to disappoint you*
Vigilance	*I learnt not to be complacent*
Invincibility	*I acquired inner strength*
Modesty	*I did not get carried away by my successes.*

Without the Soulprints that you left me, I would not have developed the PRAISE life skills model. I would not have achieved my *Break Through.* I would have had a *Rough Life* but no *Rich Life*, *Red Marks* but no *Flying Colours*...

No words can express my heartfelt love and respect for you. Your love continues to live in all these books, and in more books yet to be written and published. In gratefulness, for all your wisdom and sacrifices, I dedicate this book to you.

Thank you, Mama.

George Tan
Mother's Day
13 May 2007

最亲爱的妈妈：

一切缘于您的……

忍耐　　我扛得起千斤重担
自立　　我不坠落无望之井
自纳　　我为个人的祸福感恩
弹力　　我自强不息
决心　　我培养起追求成功的钢铁意志
毅力　　我从不绝望
诚信　　我正直不移
爱心　　我排除万难翻山越岭
自律　　我前途在握
谦卑　　我饮水思源
热心　　我重情义
骨气　　我顶天立地
坚定　　我无法让您有一丝失望
警惕　　我学会了不可自满
坚韧　　我寻获了心灵力量
朴实　　我谨记满招损、谦受益。

倘若不是您鼓励、引导我走过<<心之旅>>，我便不可能领悟、发展出 PRAISE 生活技能模式；我生命中就不会有这样的‘突破’；所经历的将只有‘穷之旅’而不是<<富之旅>>；最后惟有‘名落孙山’而不是‘再攀高峰’ – <<才之旅>>……

在我心坎深处对您的爱与敬，并非言语所能传达。您的教诲与大爱，不但留存于这几本书中，也将藉着更多将会陆续出版的创作，而在读者心中留印。缅怀着母亲您的非凡的智慧和无私精神，我谨将此书奉献给您！

谢谢您！妈妈！

水袁笔于
母亲节
2007年5月13日

inspire

Foreword

*by Jim Cathcart**

If you sincerely want something, the potential to bring it into reality already exists within you — and in those with whom you can connect.

I call this potential the "Acorn". It is the seed that has the potential to one day grow into a magnificent oak tree. The mighty oak sleeps within you right now. Water this acorn. Nurture it. One day, it will sprout. Slowly, that tiny seedling will get bigger and bigger!

---

* Jim Cathcart, CSP, CPAE is a member of the exclusive Speakers Roundtable, and is one of the top 20 motivational speakers in the world. The bestselling author of *The Acorn Principle* and *Relationship Selling*, he is also an advisor to the Schools of Business at Pepperdine University and California Lutheran University, USA.

It took me quite a while to grow my own oak tree, to fully realise my potential for achieving success and excellence in life.

When I was young, I was pretty much average. In my high school class of 430 students, I graduated somewhere around 175th. In athletics I was average as well. The only team I joined was the swimming team, and I dropped out of that before the season was fully underway.

Socially, I was again average. I had several good friends and was generally accepted by others in all the varied groups at school. But nobody encouraged me to volunteer for student leadership or nominated me for key roles in the school. In college, my pattern continued, but declined. I earned below average grades for two years in a row. Finally, I dropped out.

Somewhere along the way, however, my mindset changed. I began to realise that I could do significant things. I realised that if I really tried, I could actually be "somebody". That was when I learned how to study and how to cultivate the self-discipline I needed in order to take control of my own life.

Today, I am living my dream. I have been the president of my industry association. I have written 13 books, two of which became national bestsellers. And I have been inducted into the Speakers Hall of Fame.

I am not telling you this to impress you. I am telling you this so that you know that I know what I am talking about when it comes to the message in this book, George Tan's *SUCCESS Secrets.*

George has endured more hardships than any person should ever have to endure. Yet, he has transcended his limitations and pain to become a remarkable human being. He lifted himself from poverty and abuse to success and leadership by learning how to make things happen in his favour. You can learn this too.

George shows you how to acquire the mindset and skill sets that will bring you anything you want in life. He not only shares his methods, he also tells you the "back stories" of many of the most prominent leaders and successes in the world. You will learn how they, like George, overcame significant challenges and went on to achieve greatness.

George presents his "secrets" of success in a simple formula that he calls PRAISE, which stands for six key concepts: Prizedream, Rules, Analysis, Invincibility, Strategy and Excellence. In his reader-friendly writing style, George shows how this life skills model can be your formula for a better life.

This book is divided into two parts, titled "Inspiration" and "Life Skills". In Part I, George shares his life story and the PRAISE model for excellence and success. In Part II, he presents life stories of people who excelled in fantastic ways despite little or no formal education. While studies are undoubtedly important, what's more important is having the attitude and life skills that will help us pick ourselves up when setbacks do occur — and, from there, rise to even greater heights.

Having been a college dropout myself, I fully appreciate the tremendous value of this vital message. I know what I am talking about. So does George, who has overcome far greater difficulties and setbacks than I.

I have been inspired by this book, and I know that you will be too. Take your time and read it thoroughly. Become a successful person as you study this message. Don't just finish the book, consume it! Let its message become a part of your new thinking and actions.

This book can not only help you and those you know to become successful people, it can also help you attain the life of your dreams. It may even expand your dreams far beyond what you previously believed was possible.

There is an acorn in each and every one of us. *SUCCESS Secrets* provides the inspiration and the life skills — the water and the nutrients — to transform that acorn into a magnificent oak tree. It will help you become the person you are capable of being, and lead you to higher levels of excellence and success.

This is a must-read book about excellence and success in any educational pursuit and beyond. A greater future awaits you.

Jim Cathcart
10 October 2006

Acknowledgements

> *"We have to give every student a range of experiences from young, so that they can develop the robustness that enables them to rebound from setbacks, and the confidence to build and cross bridges in their lives."*
>
> — ***Mr Tharman Shanmugaratnam***
> ***Minister for Education, Singapore***

I am grateful to the Minister for Education, Mr S. Tharman, for these words, which he spoke at a luncheon session of the Malaysia-Singapore Roundtable. I was in the audience and his words struck me, as the cliché goes, "like a bolt of lightning".

It was 13 December 2004. I had started to write my life story about 10 weeks earlier, but had encountered numerous obstacles and was feeling very discouraged. The Minister's words struck me because my life story has been one of rebounding from setbacks. I became inspired to complete my book no matter what it took. I decided not to give up!

My mother's last wish before she died was that I should leave something behind, and I felt it would be good to share my struggles and triumphs. Recently, I came across a quotation, from the 18th-century missionary Stephen Grellet, that reaffirmed my decision to write:

> *"I expect to pass through this world but once. Any good, therefore, that I can do, or any kindness that I can show to any fellow creature, let me do it now. Let me not defer or neglect it, for I shall not pass this way again."*

I am glad that I finally got down to sharing my experiences and my success model. This dream had been at the back of my mind ever since I achieved my breakthrough and topped my professional Diploma in Personnel Management and Master of Arts in Human Resource Development at age 27.

I have many people to thank for helping me achieve my Prizedream.

I clearly remember a conversation I had in 1996 with Mr T. C. Tan, my ex-boss at National Semiconductor in 1987. He encouraged me to write my life story. I wrote 80 pages, but my story came to an abrupt stop because I was involved in another crisis. I was simply not ready then.

In August 2004, Ruth, a church friend, asked me, "What is your dream?" I said I wanted to share my tumultuous life journey with others, in the hope that they will likewise share their life stories so we can all learn from and inspire one another.

Yet, this was only a dream — I was not a writer. So where do I start?

It was the ever-helpful Professor Tommy Koh, Ambassador-at-Large at the Singapore Ministry of Foreign Affairs, who got me started (again). Ruth had mentioned my dream to him and he asked for a two-page synopsis of my life story.

That was 29 September 2004. That night, I sat down at 8 p.m. to write and did not stop until 5 a.m. I completed 30 pages. For the next 10 days, I tried and tried, but could not fit my life story into two pages. In the end, I submitted an eight-page synopsis, hoping that Prof Koh would pardon my longwindedness.

I am deeply grateful that Prof Koh took time from his busy schedule to read my synopsis, for he is a very busy man wearing many hats: Chairman of National Heritage Board, Chairman of Advisory Board of National Book Development Council, Director of Institute of Policy Studies, and many more that I may not be aware of.

Prof Koh passed my synopsis to Prof Kirpal Singh, Associate Professor of English Literature and Creative Thinking at the Singapore Management University. Both of them felt it was great for me to share my story, and asked for the manuscript.

Manuscript! It was not supposed to be part of the dream! Yet, I did not want to disappoint the two highly-respected professors, so I decided to give myself a second chance. Eight years after my aborted attempt, I decided to take on the challenge — there was to be no turning back.

Prof Singh is well-respected in literary circles for nurturing writers. I began to meet the ever-encouraging Prof Singh and to learn, from scratch, about writing, writers and the literary world.

My original plan was to write one book. Prof Singh encouraged me to write a series of books as he found my rocky life journey to be colourful. He challenged me to think big and to think outside the box. His encouragement sowed the seeds for my dream to touch the hearts of many in the old frontiers, new frontiers and lost frontiers.

This book is a result of Prof Singh's exploration and encouragement, without which I would have only written my life story, or perhaps not even that. Thanks to him advising me not to stop at one, I have so far written four other books:

- *Soulprints I — BreakThrough*
- *Benjamin Franklin — A Bright Spark!*
- *Scholars' Secrets: How to Get Your A's*
- *Rough Life Rich Life*

Another book, *Red Marks to Flying Colours* — about my successes in study, career and entrepreneurship — is on its way.

The PRAISE life skills model discussed in this book was largely inspired by Sun Zi's *The Art of War* and by my training in Naval Battle Procedure. I am grateful to the following for my navy training: RADM (Ret.) James Leo, RADM (Ret.) Kwek Swee Jin, Mr Lee Seng Kong, Mr Tan Kian Chew, Mr Gary Lee, Mr Lim Ah Seng and Mr Phillip Cheong. Without their guidance, there would have been no PRAISE model.

I am grateful to Teri Tan, correspondent for *Publishers Weekly (USA)*, for publishing an article about me in the 3 October 2005 issue. I must also thank Gregory Vijayendran of Wong Partnership and President of Rainbow Club, for his legal advice.

I am further indebted to the many international bestselling authors and top motivational speakers for their encouragement as well as their endorsements of this book and my other titles. I am touched by those who also shared their writing experiences and advice.

My ever-hardworking team of BOOKSOUL International put in their best brains and efforts to bring you this book. Thank you to the behind-the-scenes heroes who supported me, including Debbie So, Lynnette Leong, Ong Chin Ann, Charles Ban, Sheron Oh, Irene Wong, Nancy Awyong, Geraldine Ng and Ruth. Additional assistance came from Seow Hwye Tiong and Dr Tan Mei Leng of Hwa Chong Institution, Clare Lee, Chia Keng Ser, Lam Yuen Wah, Melvin Ho, Lam Yuen Chin, Ku Swee Yong, Lai Yeu Huan, Choo Boon Tiong and John Lim.

This book is an excellent example of dynamic teamwork and unswerving commitment. All these people have helped make my dream a reality. I am deeply grateful for all their insights, encouragement and generosity.

inspire

About the Author

George Tan is currently a human resource professional, change agent, head-hunter, entrepreneur, writer, publisher, hope-giver and life-long student. His passion is sharing his personal story about how he transformed his rough life into a rich life; how he kept rebounding from setbacks and never gave up.

George grew up in extreme poverty. He was badly abused by his father who was an alcoholic and an addicted gambler. He himself was a "gangster kid" addicted to gambling and the 3 V's: vulgarism, vandalism and violence.

From red marks in school, George went on to pass his postgraduate studies with flying colours. At 26, he topped his Diploma in Personnel Management. At 27, he again topped his class when he did a Master of Arts in Human Resource Development, offered as an external degree in Singapore by the US-based George Washington University. He did two programmes concurrently whilst holding a full-time job as an officer in the Republic of Singapore Navy, where he served for 10 years.

George attributes his transformation to PRAISE, a life skills model that he developed which embodies six success principles: Prizedream, Rules, Analysis, Invincibility, Strategy and Excellence. George developed the model based on his studies of Sun Zi's *The Art of War* and Naval Battle Procedure. He broadened the concepts found in these two strategy models such that they could be applied to any life situation.

Developing a life skills model and unlocking the potential of others were hallmarks of George's corporate career. He held senior human resource appointments at international corporations like Westin Hotel and the First Capital Corporation conglomerate, where he brought out the best in people.

Having reached the apex of his corporate career as Group Personnel Manager, George decided at age 35 to embark on entrepreneurship. Since then, he has successfully managed his international recruitment and head-hunting business with networks in China, India and other Asia-Pacific countries.

In 2004, at age 46, George embarked on a new life journey as a writer, publisher and hope-giver. He writes to inspire others. He believes that his life story — of overcoming tremendous odds to achieve excellence — can be an inspiration to others. He believes, too, that the PRAISE model can help others realise their dreams.

George writes to spread hope to those who, like him, might have grown up under unfavourable circumstances and have suffered setbacks in life. He writes with a simple philosophy: "*Always give yourself a second chance. Never give up!*"

Through his inspirational and motivational books, George's dream is to connect people by sharing life experiences and mutual encouragement, for the betterment of mankind.

In May 2007, George was a guest speaker at the Singapore National Community Leadership Institute. In July 2007, George addressed the 7th International Conference on Knowledge, Culture and Change in Organisation, where he shared the PRAISE model and his life story with some 250 delegates from over 40 countries, including academics and corporate executives.

George Tan's life story is featured in *Chicken Soup for the Singapore Soul*, the Singapore edition of the popular *Chicken Soup...* series of inspirational books. Through the help of many people, he is glad to have received more than 70 endorsements from top international motivational speakers and bestselling authors as well as prominent personalities in Singapore. In particular, he has received endorsements from 25 percent of the top 20 motivational speakers in the world.

He and his books have been featured in *Publishers Weekly (USA)*, 3 October 2005, and *Franklin Gazette*, the official newsletter of The Friends of Franklin, Inc, where *Benjamin Franklin — A Bright Spark!* is listed as "A Good Read".

Within Singapore, George has been featured in *The Straits Times*, *Lianhe Zaobao* and *Shin Min Daily News*, the main

English and Chinese language newspapers, as well as *'Live' 93.8*, a popular radio show.

The Sunday Times featured him in *Bookends*, a column where prominent personalities talk about the books that left an impact on their lives. George was also featured in another *Sunday Times* column, *A Life Less Ordinary.*

INWRITING, a special publication by Singapore's Ministry of Education aimed at encouraging young people to read, has reviewed *Soulprints I — BreakThrough.* George has also been featured in *NYC Times*, the newsletter of the Singapore National Youth Council.

George's books have made it to the *ST Life! Bestsellers List*, compiled by the lifestyle section of *The Straits Times*, Singapore's largest circulation English language newspaper.

Contents

1

Introduction

This book fills a vital gap present in most study and examination guides — it offers inspiration and motivation to make the student want to excel.

The importance of motivation was demonstrated early last century by Lewis Terman, a pioneer in the measurement of mental abilities. He tested a quarter of a million school children and found about 0.5 percent to be highly gifted. Terman followed up 25 years later and found, not surprisingly, that most were holding high positions in their careers. However, a number of them had become manual labourers, working as fitters, petrol-pump attendants and similar jobs. These gifted children failed to succeed in life because they lacked the urge to succeed. They lacked motivation. Terman compared them to Rolls-Royces with magnificent engines, but no petrol in the tank.

From personal experience, I can affirm that tools and techniques are useless if you lack the motivation to succeed.

It is like giving the best tools to a worker who is not motivated. He will not create anything meaningful.

Once, a social worker told me about a mother, a corporate high-flyer, who spent little time with her family. She felt bad about it and tried to compensate by giving her children lots of pocket money and the best of everything. One day, she bought her two sons the best computers, thinking it would make them study better. Instead, the boys spent their entire time playing computer games and totally neglected their studies. When she unplugged the computers, her elder son scolded her with vulgarities, while her younger son, only 11 years old, beat her until she was bruised all over — and had to seek the social worker's help.

It saddens me to hear of such stories. I sincerely hope this book can bring parents and children together to discover the source of motivation that will help the young to succeed.

Motivation has to come from within. Even young children need to motivate themselves. Parents and other family members can, however, encourage them, counsel them and offer moral support.

So, whether you buy this book as a student or as a parent, I urge you to read it with your other family members. Use this book as a platform for family bonding. Work together as a team. It will make success that much easier to achieve.

I hope my story and those of others mentioned in this book will inspire you to believe that you, or your child, can succeed no matter what the present circumstances. A summary of my story is presented in this book, and a fuller version of it can be found in my other book, *Red Marks to Flying Colours.*

I succeeded with the help of PRAISE, a life skills model that I developed from the study of strategy whilst in the navy. PRAISE provides the SUCCESS 6 Formula:

- ***S***et the ***P***rizedream. This will initiate the process of change and lead you to discover a lifetime **CHANGE** formula.
- ***U***se internal ***R***ules. When you are guided by your own internal rules, you learn to think out of the box. This gives you a lifetime **CREATIVITY** formula.
- ***C***onduct ***A***nalysis. Examine the factors that are for or against you and identify the higher cause that drives you. This is your lifetime **PASSION** formula.
- ***C***ultivate ***I***nvincibility. Acquire the virtues that lead to invincibility. These give you a lifetime **FULFILMENT** formula.
- ***E***xecute the ***S***trategy. Learn from your failures. Turn setbacks into opportunities and weaknesses into strengths. This ongoing process equips you with a lifetime **LEARNING** formula.
- ***S***ustain ***E***xcellence. Achieve it not once or twice, but over and over again in a cycle of success unlimited. Acquire a lifetime **EXCELLENCE** formula. And…

Success shall be yours, without limits.

After I topped my master's degree course, I went on to apply PRAISE in my corporate career, entrepreneurship and other life's challenges. I have been using the PRAISE model for over 20 years now and it has never failed me.

Examinations are important, but they are not as crucial as the life skills that you acquire in the process of getting those results. With the appropriate life skills in the PRAISE model, you can succeed in life even without doing well in your studies.

This book thus includes a chapter on "Famous Failures". Some did badly in school; some did not even attend school. Yet, these people have become presidents and prime ministers, Nobel Prize and Academy Award winners, millionaires and billionaires, etc.

PRAISE Books

A summary of the PRAISE model is presented in a later chapter. For an in-depth study of PRAISE, I recommend my other book, *Rough Life Rich Life,* which discusses each of the concepts in detail, with illustrations from my personal life and the lives of other great achievers.

Another series of books looks at how the greatest men and women in history — I call them PRAISE Champions — all lived by principles similar to those of the PRAISE model.

They come from diverse cultural backgrounds and achieved extraordinary success in all areas of human endeavour — conquests and politics, science and inventions, the arts, humanitarian work, and so on.

The first book in the series, *Benjamin Franklin — A Bright Spark!*, has drawn high praise from academics, scholars and fans of Franklin, many of whom feel that the PRAISE model gives interesting and important new insights into the reasons for his greatness. Roy Goodman, Curator for Printed Materials at the American Philosophical Society (which Franklin founded in 1743) and President of The Friends of Franklin, Inc., wrote in his Foreword:

> *"As America and the rest of the world celebrate the 300th birth anniversary of Franklin, there will be many books, conferences, exhibitions… However, there may not be a tribute as valuable as* Benjamin Franklin — A Bright Spark!*"*

Ralph Archbold, member of a US Federal Commission appointed by President George W. Bush and Congress to oversee the celebrations of Benjamin Franklin's 300th birthday, wrote:

> *"I have never found a book as important as this… Every person should read it and, for the sake of their future, every parent should make sure their children read it."*

Soulprints

We may never become as great as some of these PRAISE Champions. Yet, all of us can leave our imprint by making a difference in the lives of the people we encounter. When we touch people's lives in a deep and profound way, we leave imprints on their soul.

These may be called "soulprints". My mother, despite being an uneducated, illiterate woman, left me many soulprints through her love, sacrifices and wisdom. In the same way, all of us can leave soulprints in the lives of the people we touch.

You may read more of my life story in *Soulprints I — BreakThrough.* This book covered my difficult childhood, from growing up in extreme poverty and being badly abused by my father, to the time I left school. This was the period I broke free from my cycle of despair.

This book, *SUCCESS Secrets,* is therefore not a book in isolation. It forms part of a larger collection of books that will help you unlock your potential and overcome the difficulties and challenges of life in order to achieve excellence and success.

Congratulations for having this book in your hand. Your process of transformation has begun. In school, as well as in life, may you pass with flying colours!

2

Hopelessly Saddled

"You must write about Arthur."

"Arthur?" I asked, disbelievingly.

"Yes, Arthur!"

"But... He's so..."

"Lost?"

"Yes. He is such a lost soul. He is full of self-pity and arrogance. He is easily distracted, he daydreams and he is lazy. What's more, he is crippled by exaggerated fear. He said he had exam phobia!"

"Exactly. Doesn't he remind you of someone in his younger days?"

"Who? Me? You told me not to focus too much on the past!"

"But the past does hold useful lessons. Can you remember how your army and navy instructors conducted training?"

"Well, they would demonstrate how the exercise ought to be done. They would also perform a 'negative demonstration' — they purposely did it the wrong way to show how it should not be done."

"Exactly! Without darkness, would you know what is light? Without sorrow, would you know what is joy? Without being lost, would you appreciate how vital it is to have a map that shows you the way?"

Arthur had walked into my office without an appointment, just past 9 a.m. He greeted me with a bright red windbreaker, brighter red motorcycle helmet and a red-striped tie. He wore strong colours, but I found his personality weak. He was obviously talented, yet he lacked focus and direction in life.

"I see that you like red."

"*I actually like black,*" Arthur asserted, as if he needed to prove me wrong. "*But red reinforces my safety when I ride my motorbike. And red gives a strong impression when I go for a job interview.*"

He passed me his name card, which showed that he was a financial advisor with an insurance company.

"***I hope you are not asking me to buy insurance...***"

"*Selling insurance is only temporary. It gives me some pocket money. You see, I have a lot of potential that is dying to come out. Unfortunately, I have yet to find the right company that will recognise this and develop my potential to the fullest.*"

Arthur pushed his thick resume towards me. He had straight A's all the way in school, but then his grades slid and he did not qualify for the local universities. Arthur called this a "mystery".

After his National Service, Arthur pursued a four-year degree in mass communications at an American university. His father was a retired investment banker. His mother, a fine arts graduate, had stopped work to care for her children. The family was well-off.

"How did you perform at university?"

"Average, I would say. But I managed to get the degree."

Arthur clearly had talents. After his studies, he started a jazz band as well as a one-man company designing websites. He also excelled in golf and oil painting. However, his application for a US Green Card was turned down, so he returned to Singapore.

Thus began a series of job hops. He went through eight jobs in three years, but none drew out that huge hidden potential in him. Once, he quit his job after four days. As Arthur explained, "*the boss was terrible! He could not adapt to my working style at all.*" I thought it odd that an employee should expect his boss to adapt to him.

Arthur felt he should be his own boss, as only he could draw out his own potential. He convinced his father to give him $50,000 to start his own web design company. Soon after, his church pastor approached him to set up the church's website. The job later extended to setting up a music department and producing all the church's publications. After a year, Arthur suddenly realised that he was grossly underpaid for his multiple talents.

Next, Arthur got interested in real estate. One of his schoolmates was earning big money in the business. Arthur believed he could do better. But he could not make himself take the examinations to qualify as a real estate agent. He had developed an exaggerated fear of examinations since his junior college days.

So Arthur began hopping from one head-hunting firm to another, hoping to find the right employer who could draw out his great potential to the fullest.

Saddle

Once I started writing about Arthur, I felt that I should not only write about him, but I should also write for him — for all the Arthurs who are still searching to unlock their hidden potential.

These are the people that I describe as being in the "SADDLE frame of mind". They are full of **Self-pity**. They are **Arrogant**, easily **Distracted**, always **Daydreaming** and **Lazy**. They also have so-called **Exaggerated fear**. They are afraid to be tested, not just in school examinations, but in life itself. They are afraid to fail.

This fear of failure is not their fault, really. As children, they were not allowed to make mistakes. Their parents did not allow them to experiment with new things. Even when they exercised initiative or creativity, they were scolded for trying to be too smart. As a result, these children grow up afraid to take risks, afraid to do what is unconventional, afraid to fail.

When we are under SADDLE influences, we block our own paths to success. We may blame others for our failures, but the true culprit is the enemy within. SADDLE is the robber within that takes away our opportunities for excellence and success.

Like Arthur, I, too, grew up under SADDLE influences. I engaged in **Self-pity** whenever I thought about my childhood situation, and that gave me the excuse to do badly in my studies. I also behaved badly. I was a rough and tough "gangster" kid addicted to gambling and the 3 V's — vulgarism, vandalism and violence.

To the other children in the neighbourhood, I probably appeared **Arrogant**. In reality, I was feeling insecure and lousy inside.

Even as I tried to act grown up, all the little child in me wanted to do was play. I had many **Distractions**. Once, I was nearly killed because I was too distracted chasing a kite. I ran across the road without looking and, moments later, a lorry crashed into a stationary car at the exact spot where I was.

My classmates at least devoted some time to studies. I did not. I did not care if I got 22 marks for Mathematics, or 19 marks for English. In spite of this, I had **Daydreams** about entering one of the top secondary schools, but I did nothing to deserve a place.

I loved my mother. But I did very little for her when I was young. I did help her clean the school on Saturdays. But I was full of **Laziness** in my studies — the one area where my mother really wanted me to work hard and excel.

And I certainly had more than my fair share of **Exaggerated fears.** I was full of insecurities. I never had self-confidence until I topped my professional diploma when I was 26 years old. Subsequently, this new-found confidence led me to top my master's degree a year later.

Yet, I am not unique. Many others achieved success in life despite having a rough start. In fact, many overcame far greater challenges and achieved greater successes. But because my story is not as fantastic, I believe it can be a source of inspiration to those who might find it hard to relate to the really great achievers like Microsoft founder Bill Gates or Hong Kong businessman Li Ka Shing.

It is not necessary to reach their level. However small your achievement, you can consider yourself successful if you are better off than what you used to be, and if you make your own unique contribution to your family, friends and society.

Inspiration

Two weeks before I met Arthur, on 13 December, I attended a segment of the Malaysia-Singapore Forum 2004. At the event, the Singapore Minister for Education, Mr Tharman Shanmugaratnam, remarked that there had been many instances where children who did not do well academically were able to unlock their potential later in life and become very successful, especially in business.

His words struck me, as the cliché goes, like a bolt of lightning. They seeded my idea that PRAISE can be the key to unlock the potential of so many people — thousands of people struggling with finances and with life itself.

I was lucky to have PRAISE as the key that unlocked my potential. Initially, I applied some of its principles subconsciously and achieved limited success. Only when I was in my mid-20s, however, did I recognise PRAISE as a complete life skills model that can be consciously applied in a systematic way.

That was the breakthrough that turned my rough life into a truly rich one — rich in every sense of the word. Being rich does not necessarily mean having lots of money. One can, and should, also be rich in terms of learning, experiences, joy, blessings, happiness....

You, too, can turn your life around.

First, you must become aware of the SADDLE influences in your life. Then, by learning and applying the PRAISE model, you can overpower that robber and begin the process of transformation.

Congratulations for having come thus far. Your PRAISE journey — towards success unlimited — has already begun.

inspire

Part I

INSPIRATION

inspire

3

Red Marks to Flying Colours

School was a paradise for kids. Or so I thought.

"*Mama, when can I go to school?*" I must have asked my mother that question a thousand times — until the day finally came in 1965. I was seven years old and about to enter Primary 1. Then came a rude shock. In fact, a series of rude shocks . . .

My mother took me to school and to a classroom packed with more than 30 other children. Many boys and girls started to cry. Why are they crying? When will we start to play?

When class started, the teacher asked each of us to write letters of the alphabet on the blackboard. I could not even write "A". The rest of the class laughed at me.

During recess, I queued to buy noodles with the precious five-cent coin that my father had given me. When I got to the front, I was told that a bowl of noodles cost 10 cents. I was shocked and sad. I would be able to buy a bowl of noodles only every other day.

I saw a water tap at one corner of the canteen. As I drank I saw, from the corner of my eye, two kids licking rainbow-coloured ice-cream. I looked up and I saw them all. There was a long queue at the ice-cream stall. I thought ice-cream was a luxury item which only the rich could afford. These kids were taking ice-cream as freely as I took water from the tap.

I learnt a great deal at school, not about English or Arithmetic, but about the have's and have-not's. I knew my family was poor. I thought the whole neighbourhood was poor. I learnt that even among the poor, some could afford ice-cream while others could not.

Prejudice

When my younger brother, Little Emperor, went to school the following year, he was given 20 cents daily pocket money. I continued to get five cents until I reached Primary 4, when my allowance was raised to 10 cents.

My father was blatantly prejudiced against me. He hated me. He called me *suay kia*, which, in the Chinese Hokkien dialect, means "child who brings bad luck". I was his jinx.

He would cane his children whenever he was drunk, had lost in gambling, or both. Sometimes, he would strip us naked, tie us up and hang us from a ceiling hook in the living room before caning us.

These were outlets for his frustration. He was deeply frustrated because he had sailed from China to Singapore in search of the good life, but ended up earning a meagre wage as a coolie. Much later, after his death, I was to discover that he had also left behind another family in China. This obviously added to his frustration.

He would cane us until the cane split, until our skins split. He would cane his "jinx" more than any other child. Once, he produced a bunch of burning incense and poked them into my face. But he never once caned the Little Emperor, whom he loved.

Gambling and the 3 V's

When I was eight, my family moved to a neighbourhood notorious for its gangsters. And so I became a "gangster kid" addicted to gambling and the 3 V's — vulgarism, vandalism and violence.

Whenever I heard my gambling gang's special signal — the whistle from the theme music of the movie, *The Good, the Bad and the Ugly* — I would throw down my books and rush off to gamble. I would gamble even on the eve of my examinations. So, needless to say, I did badly in my studies, scoring as little as 22 marks for Mathematics, 19 marks for English.

Yet my mother constantly nagged me to become a top student. Her relatives and friends had always looked down on her because her children did badly in school. By the time I was 14, all my brothers had dropped out of school. I became my mother's last hope to redeem her years of humiliation.

Black Socks

My most traumatic experience in school, however, had nothing to do with failing examinations and disappointing my mother. It had to do with black socks . . .

"*Who says you can wear long black socks to school?*" Miss Tigress, my teacher in Primary 3, shouted at me one afternoon.

"*My white socks are still wet . . .*"

"*You mean you only have one pair of socks?*"

I nodded and decided to tell it all — about how my parents could not even afford to buy me a pair of slippers, how I had to sell my favourite pet, a champion fighting spider, to buy my own slippers, how I had just one pair of white socks . . .

Before I could even get to the part about the spider, Miss Tigress chased me out of the classroom, ordered me to take off my shoes and told me to walk round the school field until she allowed me to stop.

I walked for what seemed like hours. I was not allowed to go for my recess. During recess, hundreds of children were watching me being punished. I could hear jeers, whistles and laughter.

My self-esteem sank to its lowest. It would take me another 17 years — when I topped my class in postgraduate studies, not once but twice — before I regained my self-confidence.

Rough Life to Rich Life

The transformation of my rough life into a rich life began in Secondary 1. Most of my gambling gang had failed Primary 6 and left school. My contact with them gradually decreased.

In school, the physical education teacher was a boxing enthusiast and a good storyteller. He was my favourite teacher. He would captivate us with stories about the achievements of Muhammed Ali and other sports personalities. I was inspired to want to be like them.

Once, the teacher organised a tug-of-war. My team emerged as the champion and I was delighted. I was flattered when the teacher nicknamed me "Strong Boy". This was my first nickname that affirmed a good attribute. And I wanted to be known as a "Good Boy" too. I wanted to get rid of the 3 V's and gambling.

I decided to first tackle vulgarism. I told my friends and brothers that if they should hear a single vulgar word from me, I would have to pay them five cents. All the five cents quickly added up and I began to accumulate debts. It took me several months to pay up and to stop my vulgarism. This was a small, but important, victory for me.

Gambling was the toughest vice to give up. I finally quit the habit only several years later, when I was at pre-university.

Class Monitor

In Secondary 3, I was appointed class monitor. I felt proud to be selected. When I went home that day, I could not wait to tell my mother the good news.

"*There is nothing great to be a class monitor. Show me your excellent examination results. Better still, top the class!*" My mother's words hit me like a ton of bricks. I was shocked. She demanded only academic excellence. Nothing else would satisfy her.

I was also chosen to represent my school in badminton. With affirmations such as these, my grades improved. I rose to become the second top student in class! I told my mother, but this time without expecting any praise from her. After all, I was only the second top student in my class, not the top student in my school — which was not a prestigious school anyway. True enough, my mother was not happy. But I was.

I spent my school vacation at the library reading autobiographies of great people — Mao Zedong, Chiang Kai Shek, Suharto, Golda Meir, Josef Stalin and others. I wanted to know the secrets behind their success and greatness, but I never really learnt any secrets.

In Secondary 4, I was again made the class monitor. This time, I was elected by my class, not appointed by the teacher. It was a testimony to my leadership. I felt motivated to rise to greater heights.

I was also appointed captain of the school badminton team. I felt proud to be a "shortie" leading a team of tall badminton players! My euphoria got the better of me and I told my mother. She gave me a look of contempt! She reminded me that I was her last hope and that nothing was more important than excellent academic results.

Life Decisions

Secondary 4 was when I had to make two major decisions. First, I decided to drop one subject, Geography, and take only six subjects for the year-end GCE O-Level examinations. I wanted to focus on the other subjects as I needed only my five best subjects, including English, to qualify for pre-university.

Another, bigger decision had to do with Rachael, a foreign student who was rumoured to be a rich tycoon's daughter. She had always been nice to me. At the end of Secondary 3, Rachael invited me to spend the vacation with her in Indonesia. I turned her down because I had no money and she was visibly disappointed.

Now, Rachael dropped another bombshell. She said her parents would be sending her to the United States for further studies and that I would make her very happy if I could join her!

I was stunned. I had never thought of studying overseas. The thought of it absolutely thrilled me. Quickly however, reality got the better of me: money. As if she could read my mind, Rachael said her father had already agreed to extend a loan to me. She added that there was no condition whatsoever attached to the loan.

I could not sleep for the next few nights. I had to tell my mother about Rachael's offer.

My mother reminded me that every loan carried an obligation. She also wanted me to know that a man must be able to earn his own keep and not rely on a woman. There was nothing proud about being successful if it was due to a girl's help. A man must have "backbone".

Thus, my mother made her position very clear. I must rely on my own means if I wanted to study overseas. Otherwise, I would bring her shame, not glory. I was in a dilemma. It had become a choice between backbone and a once-in-a-lifetime opportunity.

I chose backbone. And I never saw Rachael again.

First Zero

I made it to Hwa Chong Junior College, one of Singapore's top junior colleges for pre-university studies. I was euphoric, little realising that I was about to enter the darkest period of my life.

The first signs of trouble came when I could not decide on my course of study. I started off in the Arts stream, switched to Science, switched again to Commerce, returned to Arts, before finally settling in Commerce — all within three months.

Greater trouble arose when I received a zero for a Mathematics test. It was my first zero. That was the price I paid for devoting my energy to badminton when I was already weak in my studies.

I felt depressed. I was reminded of how lousy my life had been all along. And so a study crisis escalated into a life crisis. I felt suicidal.

My way of coping with depression was to go to the beach and throw stones into the sea, each stone representing one of my troubles. I would stay at the beach till late and catch the last bus home. Many times, I did not want to go home. I wanted to walk into the water and disappear into the darkness.

One night, it dawned on me that my father's harsh treatment had made me a modern-day Spartan. He had developed in me the mental strength to pull through a crisis such as this. My mother's love was not enough. I also needed my father's toughening.

My spirits lifted when I thought that an answer had come. The navy was recruiting. I cut out the advertisement and thought each night about giving up my studies and joining the navy.

An Angel Appears

I was about to submit my application when Diana, my college mate, asked if I would like to talk to her. She had observed that I seemed troubled. I poured out all my troubles to Diana. I told her about my difficulties, especially in Mathematics, and also that I was considering quitting studies to join the navy.

Diana promised that after the examinations, she would revise all the Mathematics principles with me. With her help, I passed my Mathematics re-examination and proceeded to my second year.

I studied exceptionally hard in Pre-University 2. As my home was very noisy, I stayed back illegally in college and studied there. About 20 students were doing the same thing — until the principal conducted a series of night raids. I had a close shave.

I had to find another alternative. I decided to sleep early, at 7 p.m., and wake up to study at 2 a.m. when the rest of the family was asleep. I kept to this schedule for about six months. During this period, I was like a zombie. Some of my friends thought I was on drugs.

Smooth Sailing

I barely made it to university, but surprisingly, found university life relatively smooth sailing. For the first time, I enjoyed studying.

The only activity I joined was a study group. There were four of us in total. Each person would focus on the topic that he was strong in and brief the rest on it. We never went out for meals, movies or other recreation until after the examinations. We kept together throughout the three years of university; we never admitted new members.

I was considered one of the better students in class and I could even help the weaker students. In spite of this, my first year grades were mediocre, only two B's. My "so-so" performance was partly due to complacency, partly due to the fact that my study methods had not changed from before. I was still relying a lot on memorising and last-minute revisions.

Gradually, I improved my study methods and my grades. In my second year, I scored two A's and a "Fail" — again, due to complacency. In the third year, my grades were similar to those of the brightest member in my study group. He was offered the fourth year honours degree course, but I was not. I must have barely missed it.

I was hoping that, by improving my study methods, I would make that quantum leap to become a top student, but it did not happen. I still could not fulfil my mother's lifelong yearning. I had to wait for the next opportunity.

Flying Colours

Whilst serving as a navy captain after my university studies, I was sponsored to do a diploma in Personnel Management. In this, I discovered my passion and life vocation. At university, I had found this subject dry and boring. Now, however, my lecturers were totally practical in their focus and they helped me see Personnel Management in an entirely different light. I found it fascinating.

Whilst still pursuing the diploma programme, George Washington University offered, for the first time in Singapore as an external degree, its Master of Arts in Human Resource Development. This was no ordinary master's degree. The programme director, Professor Leonard Nadler, was regarded as the "father of human resource development".

I knew it would be tough to do two postgraduate programmes concurrently whilst holding a full-time job. I thought hard about it and decided to give myself the challenge — and the stress.

The master's programme was being offered to mature students with many years of work experience. I was a junior naval officer with minimal work experience. To gain acceptance into the course, I asked the Head Naval Personnel to write a letter of recommendation.

Next, I learnt that I absolutely needed to take leave from work during the assessment and examination periods. Skipping class was totally out of the question. In the navy, however, guaranteed leave was also totally out of the question. I could be recalled at any time for operational reasons. I thus requested to see the Commander, the highest ranking officer. My supervisor was stunned. It was like asking to see the God of Gods!

The Commander initially asked me to give up the programme. I explained the situation and I asked him to give me "moral encouragement" by granting leave as and when I needed it. He finally agreed.

I went to the course fully confident, as I was then scoring mostly A's in my diploma programme. I thought I knew exactly what to do. I was badly mistaken.

During my first individual presentation, I performed so badly that I wanted to give up. I was bombarded with many questions that I could not answer, including questions that I did not even understand. The episode left me shaken.

I was not alone in feeling the pressure. Before the first four modules of the programme were completed, six out of the original 30 students had dropped out.

My classmates, many of whom were corporate high-flyers, tended to look down on me. They would not team up with me for group projects as they feared I would drag down their scores. I had to be assigned to groups by the programme director. When I received the result for my first module, I was surprised. I got an A. But I continued to have difficulties with my classmates.

Once, I was involved in a group presentation about motivation. I hold the view that motivation has to come solely from within. Outsiders can offer incentives, but they cannot motivate. My group members would not accept my viewpoint. But when I got my report back, Prof Nadler agreed with me.

Another time, I had a group leader with a domineering personality. One day, he mentioned using "exercises" to illustrate certain learning experiences. I asked to clarify what he meant as, in the military, "exercises" involved the deployment of troops. My question annoyed him and our discussion became heated, so I requested a 10-minute break "to gain new inspiration".

During the break, the other group members commended me for having the courage to speak up. They dared not offend him. I was shocked. They were all senior corporate managers, yet they dared not speak up against a fellow classmate who had no power over us.

The course culminated in a consolidated examination that tested our familiarity with the subjects taught in the 11 previous modules. This was the ultimate test. We not only had to be familiar with all the subjects, but also with how they inter-related with one another.

A "Fail" in this paper would mean a "Fail" in the entire course. Two of my classmates did fail. So, of the 30 who joined the course, six had dropped out and two failed, leaving 22 to graduate. The two later sat for a re-examination and graduated as well.

Having persevered to do well in every module, I felt mentally prepared for the consolidated examination. There was no subject that I was weak in. I had scored A's in 10 of the 11 modules.

I passed the consolidated paper and topped my class. I did my mother proud. She achieved her Prizedream, because I had adopted it as my Prizedream.

Yet, it was not just me who passed. The PRAISE life skills model that I developed passed as well — with flying colours.

4

The SUCCESS 6 Formula

There is a difference between the "person who succeeds" and the "successful person". The person who succeeds might also fail. There is no clear pattern of success and no guarantee that he or she will recover from setbacks. A successful person, however, consistently succeeds. There is a clear pattern of success. Even if that person fails, he or she would bounce back and rise to higher levels of success.

PRAISE is a life skills model that will help develop you as a successful person. It embodies six key concepts for success:

- ***P***rizedream
- ***R***ules
- ***A***nalysis
- ***I***nvincibility
- ***S***trategy
- ***E***xcellence

Before I developed PRAISE, I made only slow and steady progress. The PRAISE model propelled me to the top and helped me stay there!

PRAISE offers what I call the **SUCCESS 6 Formula**:

- ***S***et the ***P***rizedream. This will initiate the process of change and lead you to discover a lifetime **CHANGE** formula.
- ***U***se internal ***R***ules. Learn to think out of the box. This gives you a lifetime **CREATIVITY** formula.
- ***C***onduct ***A***nalysis. Examine the factors for or against you. Find your higher cause. This is your lifetime **PASSION** formula.
- ***C***ultivate ***I***nvincibility. Acquire the virtues that lead to invincibility. These give you a lifetime **FULFILMENT** formula.
- ***E***xecute the ***S***trategy. Turn weaknesses into strengths, setbacks into opportunities. This is your lifetime **LEARNING** formula.
- ***S***ustain ***E***xcellence. Achieve it over and over again in a cycle of unlimited success. Acquire a lifetime **EXCELLENCE** formula.

Success shall be yours, without limits.

Before we apply PRAISE, we must watch for the six negative influences that spell out the word SADDLE:

- ***S***elf-pity
- ***A***rrogance
- ***D***istractions

- ***D***aydreams
- ***L***aziness
- ***E***xaggerated fear

SADDLE influences block our path to excellence and success.

Prizedream

The Prizedream is the true motivator. It is a desire so strong that you will do whatever it takes to make it come true, including working hard and making sacrifices. It is so valuable that you will never give up trying to achieve it. True, you might feel discouraged along the way. But you will always find renewed strength.

The Prizedream is the beginning of change. All change begins with a vision. The Prizedream provides us with a lifetime **CHANGE** formula.

Do not worry about having to work hard and struggle — the key is motivation. Once you are motivated, you will view hard work and struggle differently and you will come to not mind them at all. Some students are able to study late into the night and, more importantly, to study consistently throughout the year. Others might think that they are struggling. But if the student is

> The Prizedream is not a wish. If you merely wish to do well in your studies, you simply wait for it to happen. This is not much different from waiting to win the lottery — it is a daydream. Once you are motivated to put in your blood, sweat and tears to make your wish come true, it becomes a Prizedream!

working towards a Prizedream, perhaps to win a scholarship, then it is not a struggle.

Of course, the body has its limits and there will come a time when, no matter how big your Prizedream, you will feel the strain. You need to take a break and rest.

If you are realistic about achieving your Prizedream, you will adopt a balanced approach to keep your body healthy and your mind alert. You will take care to avoid stress and emotional upsets, and not push yourself to the point of exhaustion.

Dream big, start small

"To those of you who received honours, awards and distinctions, I say 'Well done'. And to the C students, I say: 'You, too, can be president of the United States.'"

— George W. Bush, US President

"You see things; and you say, 'why?' But I dream things that never were; and I say, 'Why not?'"

— George Bernard Shaw, playwright

The prize or reward must be big enough to motivate you to work hard, yet not be so big that the very thought of it frightens you and makes you give up before even trying. For example, if you are currently failing in school, the thought of becoming a top student or winning a scholarship may be too big a Prizedream.

So set yourself a smaller Prizedream first. Aim to pass your examinations. When you are able to pass, aim to do well. Then once you are able to do reasonably well, aim to excel.

Dream big. But start small. Set the big dream aside. Leave it at the back of your mind. One day, you will be ready for it.

Prizedreamers

Agnes Gonxha Bojaxhiu had a small Prizedream: to serve "the poorest of the poor". Her pursuit of this humblest of dreams made her one of the most highly respected and best loved women of modern times, better known as **Mother Teresa.**

Cliff Young was never too old to have a Prizedream. As a 61-year-old potato farmer, he dreamed of winning the 1983 inaugural Sydney-Melbourne Ultra Marathon, a race that would cover 875 km and be subsequently hailed as one of the world's greatest running races.

Instead of running, he "shuffled" in a half-run, half-walk gait. He was laughed at, jeered at and thought to be crazy. Yet he not only won the race, beating 149 world-class athletes, but won it by a staggering nine hours!

(*Continued*)

(*Continued*)

Paulo Coelho is the Brazilian author of *The Alchemist,* a book described as "a fable about following your dreams". Yet, he nearly abandoned his own Prizedeam.

On the eve of his 30th birthday, Coelho gave up his dream of becoming a writer. He was, at that time, both successful and happy as a music producer. The next morning, he was fired with no reasons given. For the next two years, he could not find a similar job.

Thus, he returned to writing. *The Alchemist* became one of the most successful books of modern times. To date, Coelho has published 15 book titles, with 380 translations and worldwide sales of over 75 million copies. A Reuters news report in 2003 named Coelho as one of the three most successful authors today.

Rules

"I don't go by the rule book. I lead from the heart, not the head."

— Princess Diana, Princess of Wales

"There are no rules here, we are trying to accomplish something."

— Thomas Edison, inventor

"Rules are not necessarily sacred. Principles are."

— Franklin D. Roosevelt, former US President

Rules are commonly viewed as external rules imposed upon us — school rules, the laws of a country, social norms and so on. Thus, many people dislike rules. They feel that rules restrict freedom and stifle creativity.

But rules are meaningful. What would soccer be like if the game is played without rules? What would tennis, badminton, chess, Scrabble, or any other sport or game be like? We enjoy these games because there are rules.

Rules also force us to think of creative solutions. When we are restricted by rules, and have to find solutions within those restrictions, we become truly creative.

The *haiku*, a form of verse that originated in Japan, has very restrictive rules. It is written in three lines, with five syllables in the first line, seven in the second, and five in the third. This requires more creativity than writing any number of words, in any style.

Thus, rules provide us with a lifetime **Creativity** formula.

Internal rules

We also have rules that we impose upon ourselves. These are our internal rules. Often, they are more important than the external rules, because our internal rules have a greater bearing on our lives.

Everyone has internal rules about punctuality. Maybe your rule is that it is okay to be 10 minutes late. For another person, the internal rule is that he must be on time. So if you turn up 10 minutes late, the other person will be upset, as your internal rules are different. We have our own rules about everything — about honesty, punctuality, courtesy, respect, friendship, money, work and so on.

So what are your rules? Do your rules help you achieve your goals in life? Do they help you become who you want to be?

Let's say you want to do well in your studies, but your internal rules say it is okay to relax and take things easy. Will you do well? Not likely. If you want to do well, you need to change your internal rules.

The PRAISE model recommends these five internal rules:

- Be different
- Be decisive
- Take control
- Never give up
- Take ownership

When we live by these five internal rules, we can overcome many obstacles in life, including obstacles presented by external rules.

Be different

If you look around you, you will see that most people are average. Whether you are in school, college, university or doing postgraduate studies, it is usually the same case.

Look also at your own life up to now. Have you also been average?

If you want to excel, you need to be different from what you used to be; you need to be different from most other people. If you always studied at the last minute, try studying consistently throughout the year. If you always kept quiet during class discussions, try taking on a more active role. If you always study late at night, try going to sleep early and studying in the morning. If you always study alone, see if joining a study group can be helpful.

There is no single way that suits everyone. But if what you had been doing did not help you, then you need to find another way.

Being different also means daring to go against norms and expectations. If you come from a family of doctors, will you study medicine simply because it is expected of you? Do you dare to study something different?

Don't be different just for the sake of being different. Search yourself deeply and ask, is this what you really want? Will you be willing to accept the difficulties when they arise? If your answer is yes, by all means go ahead. Follow your passion.

In your soul searching, you might also realise that you had merely been entertaining some fanciful daydreams. In that case, you would do well to return to reality — and follow the crowd!

> When you seek to be different, do it for a good reason.

The Fosbury Flop

American high jumper **Dick Fosbury** found the existing high jump techniques to be too complicated. So he developed a new, radically different technique. He jumped backwards!

As a university student, Fosbury won the National Collegiate Athletic Association championships in 1968. That same year, he created a sports sensation when he won the gold medal at the Mexico Olympics and set a new Olympic record.

Today, almost all high jumpers use his technique. Despite its success, the technique is called, ironically, the Fosbury Flop!

Be decisive

Being decisive does not mean being hasty in making decisions. By all means, evaluate the situation properly before you decide. Once you have decided, be firm. Do not waver. Do not turn back — unless, of course, you realise you made a wrong decision. Once you have decided, there is no way of knowing "what if. . ." So don't fret over it. Make the best of your decision.

Indecisiveness is only natural when you are faced with a major turning point in life, such as when you have to decide what subjects to study, because that will decide your career and your life.

So yes, you may need to gather information and consult people in order to make an informed and well-considered decision. But there can be no end to this. You can keep finding out more information, keep hearing more opinions, until you become totally confused. At some point, you need to decide and move on. You will feel much better once you have decided — no matter what the decision is.

Top golfer **Tiger Woods** was decisive when he changed his golf swing — the single most important factor that determines a golfer's performance. Woods made the change in 2003 and had a disappointing year that season. In 2004, he slipped to the No. 2 spot and even fell briefly to No. 3.

However, Woods did not waver in his decision. He felt he had a fault in his technique and was playing well in spite of it. Then he made a spectacular comeback. By end-April 2005, Woods had regained his No. 1 spot. At the time of writing, in October 2006, Woods was still firmly in the top spot.

Take control

To take control means to create your own outcomes, rather than letting others decide what should happen to you.

Two groups of people have influence over your life. The first group is made up of those in positions of power and authority, such as the government, school principal, teachers and parents. For instance, the government decides which system of education the citizens of the country must follow. Some people who disagree migrate so that their children can undergo a different educational system. They thereby take control.

Another group of people that might have an influence over your life, even though they may have no real power over you, are those who make up "the environment", such as your family and friends.

My home environment was very noisy, so I sought alternative solutions to study. At first, I joined a group of friends in staying illegally overnight at the college. Later, I tried sleeping at 7 p.m. and waking up at 2 a.m. to study. I took control. I did not allow my family members to affect my studies.

At university and even in secondary schools, a student's work may involve team projects. Such teams are usually assigned by the teacher, so as a student, you may not have control over who you work with. However, you can still take control by assuming a leadership position. Even if you are not the team leader, you can participate actively in team discussions and decision making. This way, you can steer the direction of the team.

When you form your own study groups, you can choose the people whom you know (or believe) to be reliable. You can delegate tasks and feel confident that the group members will do a good job. This way, you take control without having to do the job yourself.

Actress **Michelle Yeoh,** known for her action films, believes in taking control. She performs nearly all the stunts in her films.

This has earned her the highest respect from top film directors, producers and fellow movie stars on both sides of the Pacific — in Hollywood and Hong Kong. It also landed her top roles, such as in the James Bond movie, *Tomorrow Never Dies,* and the award-winning Chinese martial arts film, *Crouching Tiger, Hidden Dragon.*

Never give up

"Many of life's failures are men who did not realise how close they were to success when they gave up."

— Thomas Edison, inventor

My masters degree course started off with 30 students. Before the first four (out of 11) modules, six students had given up and dropped out. Among those who stayed on, there might have been others who "gave up" indirectly by not putting in their best effort. My classmates were corporate high-flyers with strong credentials. There was no reason for any of them to fail. Yet, two of them did.

Two things helped me cultivate the "never give up" spirit. One was my father's harsh treatment of me when I was young, which strengthened my will. Other forms of difficulty, such as military or intensive sports training, can have a similar effect.

Another, physically less demanding, factor came from reflection and inspiration. As I sat by the beach throwing stones into the sea, I observed the waves come and go. As one wave receded, another came forward. They seemed to be telling me never to give up.

There may be times when you have made wrong decisions. But do not give up at the first signs of obstacles and setbacks. When you persevere in the face of setbacks, you will realise that they often provide valuable lessons for future challenges.

Probably the most remarkable example of a person who never gave up in the face of rejection was **Harland David Sanders**. At 65, he was almost penniless as he travelled across the US to sell an idea that he had. He slept in his car to save money. Over a two-year period, he was rejected 1,008 times before the 1,009th person said "Yes".

If the name Sanders sounds familiar, it is because he is none other than "Colonel Sanders", founder of Kentucky Fried Chicken.

Take ownership

Taking ownership means accepting responsibility for the outcome of your decisions and actions. It means not blaming others when things go wrong, while giving credit when things go right.

If you have a habit of blaming others, you are giving them control over your life. Thus, if you are not happy, it is because your parents/teachers/classmates made you unhappy. If you are not successful, again, it is the fault of someone else.

Intel CEO

In a dramatic display of taking ownership, **Craig Barrett,** Chief Executive Officer of Intel Corp, got down on his knees during an industry conference in October 2004 and begged forgiveness for the company's poor performance.

Shares of Intel had lost 34 percent of their value during the year. Barrett admitted that the company's managers had become "too relaxed" and that management missteps had caused five projects to be scrapped or delayed.

My younger brother never learnt to take ownership of his failure in school. When he failed his examinations, my father blamed me for not setting him a good example. Later, my father hired tutors for him. When he again failed, it became the tutors' turn to get blamed.

It is natural to be influenced by other people. At university, I tended to do better when I found the lecturers interesting compared to when I found the lecturers boring. However, other students could do well no matter how interesting or boring the lecturers were.

If I want success, I have to create it for myself. Others can assist me, just as those lecturers who livened up their classes with stories and jokes had assisted me. But I cannot depend on them. I must be able to create my own success.

When I received my first A in my master's programme, I bought myself an expensive badminton racquet. That was my way of recognising my own achievement. It was my way of taking ownership.

Analysis

Analysis considers those factors that either help or obstruct your Prizedream. It looks at your gifts and talents, strengths and weaknesses, and also at how you lead others and manage your resources.

Some of these factors are within your control, such as the books you read or the friends you choose to spend time with. But even when other factors — such as physical disabilities — are beyond your control, you might still be able to minimise their effects.

Analysis helps you discover the higher cause or inspiration that drives you forward. This is your passion. Thus, through analysis, you discover a lifetime **PASSION** formula.

Analysis helps in decision making. When I decided in Secondary 4 to drop Geography, it was the result of my analysis. Although Geography was one of my favourite subjects, I saw that it required a lot of memorising of facts, which was not my strong point.

Often, people already have their minds made up, and if their analysis tells them that they had made a poor decision, they either ignore or play down the results of such analysis. This is not entirely wrong. Just because your analysis tells you that there will be problems ahead, it does not mean that you should abandon your plans. All it means is that you have to work harder, so that when the difficulties arise, you will face them fully prepared.

A good analysis will not only reveal your strengths and weaknesses, but also where they come from. Perhaps you draw strength from exercise, eating healthy foods, visiting the beach, sleeping early, or from prayer, meditation and other spiritual practices. You feel good when you do such things. Do you do them often enough?

When you analyse your weaknesses, you might also find out if they can be overcome. If you are weak in languages or at remembering facts and figures, is there anything you can do to improve yourself?

What if you have a weakness that cannot be overcome? Well, you can choose a life path where your weaknesses do not matter. If you are extremely weak in your studies, are you doomed? Of course not! You can still be a sportsman, an artist, a chef, even a businessman.

Focus on strengths

> *"We must look for the opportunity in every difficulty instead of being paralysed at the thought of the difficulty in every opportunity."*
>
> — ***Walter E. Cole, Korean War hero***

While you analyse your strengths and weaknesses, focus on your strengths. This does not mean that you should ignore your weaknesses. You need to know your weaknesses and try to eliminate them. Weaknesses, however, give you plenty of excuses. You may start to say, "Oh, I cannot do this and I cannot do that because I am weak." When you focus on your strengths instead, you will stop giving yourself excuses and start to say, "I can do it!"

The sky's the Limit

New Zealand mountaineer **Mark Inglis** did not focus on his weakness — the fact that he has no legs. Both his legs were amputated below the knee in 1982 after suffering frostbite when he was trapped for 14 days in an ice cave.

(*Continued*)

(*Continued*)

In May 2006, Inglis became the first person to reach the top of Mount Everest, the world's highest peak, with two artificial legs. Even when one of his artificial legs broke, Inglis shrugged off the mishap as "a minor hiccup".

Singaporean mountaineer **David Lim**, likewise, did not focus on his weakness. In 1998, Lim was stricken with Guillain–Barre Syndrome, a rare nerve disorder that left him paralysed from the eyes down. He spent six months in hospital and became partially disabled in both legs. In 1999, Lim resumed mountain climbing. Today, he is one of Singapore's most active mountaineers, with more than 50 high mountain ascents.

Another person who pushed his limits, literally to the sky, is British teenager **Daniel Reilly**. In 2005, at the age of 18, he started his own airline, operating out of his bedroom! Daniel explained: "The idea of setting up my own airline started as a joke when my friends said I should charge to fly people around. I put together a business plan and contacted a financial adviser and now it is really happening."

In the PRAISE model, Analysis is adapted from the teachings of Sun Zi in *The Art of War*. Sun Zi advises us to analyse the following five factors:

- Cause
- Heaven
- Earth
- Command
- System

These may sound abstract at first, but as we apply them to real-life examples, you will see that they are in fact very practical.

Cause

This is the inspiration — the higher reason — that motivates a person. If you want to do well in your studies, ask yourself: what is the higher cause that drives this desire? Why do you want to excel?

When I was a playful child who strove to become "king" of various games, my Cause was to develop a sense of self-worth. I was very weak in my studies, so I tried to make up for it by excelling in games. Later, I set myself a new target — to become a top student in my postgraduate studies. I wanted to do it for my mother. I wanted to redeem the years of humiliation that she suffered when relatives and friends looked down on her. My mother was my Cause.

My mother had wanted me to be a top student all along. Now, I wanted to do it. I wanted to make up for all the times when I disappointed her. This was a crucial difference. Even though my mother was my Cause and inspiration, I myself wanted to do well.

When a city bids to host a major event like the Olympic Games, the Cause might be to revive the city, to give it new life, boost the economy and bring it prestige and glory. This, however, is merely the Cause of the host city. In 2005, London won the bid to host the 2012 Olympics because it spelt out a greater, higher Cause — to revive interest in sports among young people. This was a Cause that the entire Olympic movement could identify with.

Heaven

Heaven may sound abstract at first, but think about what Heaven is. It is simply the larger external environment that we cannot change.

We cannot change the Heavens, nor can we change the sun, the moon, the stars and the weather. But we can understand Heaven and prepare ourselves to cope better with it. If it is going to rain, we cannot stop the rain, but we can be ready with our umbrellas and raincoats.

The education system is not something that you can easily change. If you really want, you can study abroad, but this is not easy. Likewise, it is not easy to change your teachers. If they speak in a boring manner, you just have to make the best of the situation.

What about your level of intelligence? Is it a fixed, Heaven factor, or can it be improved upon? This is a complex issue. There are different ways to measure intelligence — IQ tests, examination results, career success, and so on. My observation is this: many people seem to stay at the same level — below average, average, or above average — throughout their lives. But some do manage to achieve major breakthroughs. In my case, I improved gradually and achieved my breakthrough when I did my postgraduate studies.

There are also people who can improve overnight after attending self-improvement and mind development workshops. I know of one child who improved her grades in Chinese language from fail to distinction through hypnotherapy! It may not be that the person actually becomes more intelligent, but more likely that certain mental blockages were removed. It has at least unlocked her hidden potential.

The 26 December 2004 tsunami was a tragic case of people being unprepared for Heaven forces. Luckily, there was one young English schoolgirl on holiday in Phuket, Thailand, who had just learnt about tsunamis in her Geography lesson. When the sea suddenly receded, she understood what it meant and warned the people around her to run to higher ground. They were saved. The Geography lesson was the girl's Heaven factor, while the girl's presence was a Heaven factor for those around her.

For the many others who went down to the beach to check out why the sea had suddenly dried up, their ignorance was their Heaven factor. Unfortunately, it resulted in their tragedy.

Thus, Heaven factors have a certain element of "luck". If your favourite topic comes out as an examination question, that is your good luck. But if you know that the examiner likes a certain topic and you prepare for it, and it gets asked as an examination question, that is your initiative. There is not much you can do about your luck, but there is a lot you can do about your preparedness and initiative.

Matsushita's "Luck"

Konosuke Matsushita grew up in poverty. He received limited education and, at age 9, had to leave his family to work in another city. When he was in his early 20s, he developed a serious lung illness and was advised by his doctors to rest for at least six months, but he could not afford that luxury.

When Matsushita first set up his own company, Matsushita Electric, business was so bad that he nearly went bankrupt. After the Second World War, the company was slapped with severe restrictions imposed by the Allied Forces.

Yet, Matsushita always considered himself lucky. He not only accepted his fate, but always saw the positive

(*Continued*)

(*Continued*)

side of it. This is the spirit that helped him transform his tiny electrical workshop into one of the world's biggest manufacturers of electrical appliances, known throughout the world today by its brand names that include National and Panasonic.

Earth

Unlike Heaven, we can change the Earth. We can flatten the land, clear the forest, build roads, plant trees, build dams, create lakes, divert waterways, and so on.

In the PRAISE model, Earth refers to the immediate operating environment and the resources available that may be within our control. It includes our family, social and working environments. These are factors we can change, or at least adapt to.

If your family environment does not support you in achieving your goals, you can work harder to enlist their support, or you can also "leave" your family temporarily. This may not be as drastic as it sounds. For example, if your home is noisy, you can go elsewhere to study. This is equivalent to temporarily "leaving" your family.

Earth also refers to the social environment such as your network of friends, who can have a profound impact on you. At university, one of my classmates who did well in pre-university and in the officer cadet's course in the navy, failed because he was constantly engaged in boy/girl relationships.

Of course, the impact could be just as great the other way around. One girl I know started off as an average student, but because her boyfriend was one of the top students, her grades improved and she ended up with a First Class Honours degree.

Command

Command refers to the leader's ability to lead and inspire others. What has this to do with studies? First, you need to "command" yourself. You need to impose self-discipline so that you won't be distracted or lazy.

In general, whenever someone forces you to do something, your natural response will be to resist. Likewise, when you force yourself, you will also resist. Therefore, you need to find a way to inspire yourself. Lead, don't force, yourself to study. Then you will do it willingly and happily.

How? Focus on your Prizedream. Think of the prize, the reward, that comes from studying hard and doing well. Alternatively, focus on your Cause, the higher reason that drives your passion.

Command is also important when you interact with fellow students, whether in group projects or in informal study groups. You need not be officially appointed as a group leader. You can "lead" by being active in the group discussions, proposing good ideas, or volunteering for certain tasks instead of waiting to be assigned. You can also "lead" by asserting your rights as a member of the group, and not allowing the official leader to dominate unnecessarily.

Florence Nightingale is famous for helping wounded soldiers during the Crimean War in 1854 and for modernising the nursing profession. At the hospital in Scutari, where she worked during the war, she was constantly obstructed by bureaucrats and doctors who were reluctant to help her. When she led a team of 38 nurses to Scutari, several of them gave up upon arrival when they saw the deplorable conditions there.

Despite such obstacles, she vastly improved the conditions of the hospital, as well as the survival rate of patients. This was possible because she managed to secure allies who supported her cause. It shows the strength of her Command.

System

System refers to a person's competence in managing direct and indirect resources to achieve a Prizedream. If your Prizedream is to do well in studies, such resources might include books and other sources of information, teachers, helpful friends, and so on.

The one resource that everyone needs to manage is time. It's not how much time you have, but how effectively you use it. You can spend hours reading up on a subject and still not understand it, during which your time would have been wasted. Alternatively, you can discuss the subject with a friend and find that, within a few minutes, you are able to understand it well. Thus, your time would have been well spent.

You may also find that if you study a few hours at a stretch, your mind becomes tired. But if you take short breaks every now and then, your mind may be fresher and you can study better. You may even find that walking away from your task — whether you are reading a book, writing an assignment or solving a problem — will cause inspiration to arise.

> Managing your time is not just about managing the hours and minutes. It is also about managing your mental alertness, energy level and other factors that determine what you achieve in that time.

You also need to think about the indirect resources that might be available to you. For instance, is it true that everyone has the same 24 hours in a day? Not really. If you have family members or friends helping you study — by picking up books from the library, making photocopies and performing other mundane tasks — you are, in fact, using their time.

Others can even "study" on your behalf. In my study group at university, each of us would study our strong subjects in great depth, and then brief the rest when we met. This way, we saved time. We could do this because all four of us were serious and committed. We knew we could depend on each other.

Books are also important resources. The books that your teachers recommend may well be "the best". But if you find them difficult to understand or uninspiring, why not read others? If reading a basic book helps you understand a subject, that is better than reading "the best" book and not understanding it.

Finally, the Internet can be a vast source of information for today's students, provided you know how to use it well. Recently, one of my friends needed to check some historical data about Singapore. After searching both the Internet and printed materials for two days, my friend gave up as she could not find the information she wanted. When another friend learnt about this, he went to the Internet and found the information within two minutes.

Of course, the Internet is not always a reliable source of information, so you will need wisdom to discern which information can be trusted and which cannot.

We will look more at wisdom in a later chapter. For now, you need to realise that, as a student, you actually have quite a vast pool of resources at your disposal. Learn to manage these resources well.

As leader of London's bid team for the 2012 Olympics, **Sebastian Coe** persuaded influential ambassadors to

(*Continued*)

(Continued)

join the team, including other Olympians, football star David Beckham and former South African President Nelson Mandela.

Coe also created a new resource comprising more than 30 youths aged 12 to 18, and focused his presentation around the young. He spoke about getting young people interested in sports instead of video games and junk foods. This turned out to be London's secret weapon at its presentation.

Invincibility

"If I have to, I can do anything. I am strong, I am invincible, I am Woman."

— ***Helen Reddy, singer***

"Inner strength can overcome anything that occurs outside."

— ***I Ching***

"People do not lack strength; they lack will."

— ***Victor Hugo, writer***

When I did my diploma and masters degree programmes, my attitude was totally different from my younger days in school. When I was younger, I viewed myself as a lousy student. This time round, I saw myself as having the potential to become a top student. I also believe that the PRAISE model gave me the tools to excel.

Invincibility is partly about having confidence and the winning attitude. This is very important. While confidence would not guarantee success, lack of confidence certainly guarantees failure. Invincibility is also about cultivating leadership qualities. In Sun Zi's *The Art of War,* these qualities are called the virtues of a general.

What has this to do with studies and examinations? At first, it may not seem much. But these qualities are important for everyone in every situation, including students, as they build your strength of character. They give you an inner strength so that external challenges and difficulties won't get you down. They help you rebound from setbacks and even failures. As a result, you will not be easily defeated. Eventually, you will triumph.

According to Sun Zi, the five virtues of a general are:

- Wisdom
- Sincerity
- Courage
- Strictness
- Benevolence

These five virtues bring us a life of fulfilment. Cultivating invincibility thus helps us discover a lifetime **FULFILMENT** formula.

Note that "general" does not have to mean a military commander. Everyone is a general. As a student, you are a general in charge of yourself, your studies and your assignments. If you work on a group project, you might also be the general in charge of the group. You could be appointed team leader by the teacher-in-charge, or you could naturally assume a leadership role.

In school, you could also be the captain of a sports team, commander of a uniformed group, or leader of a music group. All of us are generals in one way or another. Thus, all of us would do well to cultivate the five virtues.

Wisdom

In this Information Age, knowledge is easy to come by. If you need to know about something, just do an Internet search. You will likely find lots of information about it, even if it is an obscure subject. You might also find contradictory and false information. Thus, you need wisdom to know which information to accept, and which to reject.

Wisdom is not just about knowledge and understanding. These qualities will obviously help you in your studies and examinations. But more than that, you need to know what is true and what is right in order to make good judgements.

Let's say you planned to spend the night studying, but your friends invite you out. Should you go? Or say you feel tired and sleepy. Should you take a break, or force yourself to study? There is no fixed rule for such situations. Sometimes, you really do need a break, but you also need to discipline yourself. With wisdom, you will know when to push yourself, and when to relax.

Wisdom does not always come from school education. It comes more from having experienced life and from listening to the advice of people, usually the elderly, who have the experience.

My Mother's Wisdom

One of the wisest persons in my life was **my mother**. She was uneducated and illiterate, yet most of the time, she knew what was the right thing to do. Her wisdom kept the family together and our stomachs full, in spite of our financial hardships.

As a young student, you may not have a lot of life experiences. But you learn along the way. You may find, for example, that every time you give yourself a break, you end up taking a much longer break than you intended. Or that every time you force yourself to study no matter how tired you are, you end up not being able to concentrate.

Such experiences should help you strike a good balance between forcing yourself and taking things easy. You learn from your experiences and mistakes, and gain in wisdom.

Investment guru **Warren Buffett** is highly intelligent, well-educated and enormously wealthy, and also displays a great deal of wisdom.

Buffett started young in acquiring wisdom. He made his first stock purchase when he was 11 years old, buying City Securities' preferred shares for $38 each, and selling them when the price hit $40. The price later skyrocketed to $200. This taught him the wisdom of investing in the long-term.

Fast forward to 2006 — at age 75, Buffett has become the second richest man in the world, with a personal wealth estimated by *Forbes Magazine* at US$42 billion.

In June 2006, Buffett made the single largest donation in the history of philanthropy when he pledged to give away about US$37.4 billion. But instead of starting his own charity foundation, Buffett decided to donate his money to a foundation that would be well-managed. The bulk of his wealth, about US$31 billion, would go to the Bill and Melinda Gates Foundation, founded and managed by the richest man in the world, Bill Gates.

Bill Gates, at 50, is 25 years younger than Buffett. He has announced his decision to give up the day-to-day operations of Microsoft Corporation and focus on philanthropic work instead. Buffett thus recognised that his

(*Continued*)

(*Continued*)

money would go a longer way in the hands of Bill and Melinda Gates. While his gesture is widely regarded as a sign of great benevolence, the way he went about it demonstrates his great wisdom.

Sincerity

For students, sincerity obviously means not cheating in assignments or examinations. It goes beyond that, however, and covers your daily interactions with teachers and fellow students as well. Most of all, you need to be sincere with yourself.

During my second year at pre-university, I learnt an important lesson about sincerity and truthfulness. I had stayed overnight at the college illegally to have a quiet place to study. There were about 20 students who stayed back, but not all were studying. Some spent almost the entire time playing games. Although I was good at the games, I pretended that I did not know how to play them since I really wanted to study.

One night, a friend confronted me and asked if I really did not know how to play the various games. I hesitated. Because of that, he already knew the truth. So I told him. His eyes lit up when I said I was good at a Chinese game of strategy called *zong si ling*, or "general", as that was considered one of the most difficult games of all.

I thought he would be angry with me for previously hiding the truth, but instead, he admired my determination and felt inspired. He decided to follow my example and stop playing games.

Abraham Lincoln, who is widely regarded as the greatest American president of all time, stood out for his personality and strength of character more than anything else. Not that his accomplishments were minor — on the contrary, they were very major. Lincoln preserved the unity of the United States of America by leading the government to victory in an American Civil War (1860–1864). He also ended slavery in the US, granting freedom to some four million African-Americans.

However, Lincoln was so loved for his integrity and sincerity that his most popular nickname is Honest Abe. In 1831, while working as a storekeeper, he once walked more than six miles to return six and a half cents that he had inadvertently overcharged a customer. Another time, he walked several miles to return four ounces of tea because he discovered he had given a customer the wrong amount.

Lincoln once told a friend that his religious code was the same as that of an old man he knew: "When I do good, I feel good, and when I do bad, I feel bad, and that's my religion."

Courage

Are you afraid of your teachers and lecturers? Are you even afraid of some of your classmates? Do you have the courage to answer questions without being asked? Or are you afraid of appearing foolish if you give the wrong answer?

The greatest courage involves facing yourself, being responsible for yourself and ultimately, being yourself. This is moral courage.

At pre-university, I saw how a lack of moral courage landed one of my college mates, Heng, in trouble. Heng was active in sports. He exuded confidence and I always had the impression that he was an excellent student. However, he failed Physics and Chemistry and had to repeat his first year.

Heng told me he could not face his parents. He had been a good student throughout secondary school. However, because he came from a Chinese school, he struggled with his lessons at pre-university. He did not have the courage to tell his parents, or anyone else, about this. Instead, he kept up the impression that he was coping well.

When Heng's parents found out that he had failed, they proved to be understanding. Heng felt a great burden lifted off his chest. He was thus able to focus on his studies and pass in the end.

Heng's story holds an important lesson. Often, we are afraid to reveal the truth because we worry that others might react negatively. But when they see that we are genuinely facing difficulties and that we sincerely want to do well, they will usually be understanding. Even if they were to react negatively, any unpleasantness would most likely be short-lived. It is better to just bear with it than to carry the burden of having to hide the truth.

Nelson Mandela spent 27 years in prison for his armed struggle against apartheid in South Africa. Once considered a terrorist, Mandela was actually a firm believer in non-violence and had taken up the armed struggle as a last resort.

Upon his release from prison in 1990, he pursued a policy of reconciliation and this set the stage for a smooth transition to democracy. In 1994, he became the first President of South Africa to be elected in fully representative democratic elections.

Mandela retired from the Presidency in 1999. As an elder statesman, Mandela continues to voice his opinions on a number of topical issues. In 2003, Mandela insinuated that US President George W. Bush might have been racist in not following the United Nations on the issue of the War in Iraq, because UN Secretary-General Kofi Annan was a black man. Mandela's comments stirred controversy and led to criticisms from even his supporters. Yet, he was not afraid to speak his mind.

(*Continued*)

(*Continued*)

John Robbins, author of *Diet for a New America*, is another person not afraid to speak up. Robbins was the heir to Baskin-Robbins, the world's largest ice-cream empire founded by his father and uncle in 1945. His home even had a swimming pool in the shape of an ice-cream cone!

However, Robbins gave this all up to write books about the cruel treatment of farm animals and the harmful effects of eating meat and dairy products — including ice-cream! In doing so, he not only went against his family, but also against the powerful, multi-billion-dollar meat and dairy industries. He did it because he believed it was the right thing to do. He did it because he had moral courage.

Strictness

"In reading the lives of great men, I found that the first victory they won was over themselves — self-discipline with all of them came first."

— Harry S. Truman, former US President

Personal victory is the most important victory that must be won. It comes first and foremost. Before you can gain victory over someone else or over a situation (such as your examination), you need to gain victory over yourself. This comes with self-discipline, or strictness.

Strictness strengthens character and helps us succeed. When you look at the lives of successful people, you will find that they all impose strict codes on themselves. Such codes might concern the allocation of time, such as setting aside time to study, or they might involve daily routines such as daily exercises or meditation.

If, as a student, you are able to adhere to a strict routine, you will set aside enough time to study and find that you still have time for recreational activities to provide balance to your life. In my third year of university, I stayed at the student hostel and part of the routine there was to set aside 5 p.m. to 7 p.m. for recreation and dinner. I found this routine to be very useful as it helped me plan the rest of my day. More importantly, the hostel routine helped me stick to my personal routine.

Benjamin Franklin, a founding father of the United States of America as well as a great scientist, inventor, entrepreneur and writer, was a master of self-discipline. At age 20, he drew up a list of 13 virtues in order to "live without committing any fault at any time". But more important than drawing up the list, he also drew up a plan to achieve it. He marked the start of each day with

(*Continued*)

(*Continued*)

the question: "What good shall I do today?" And at the end of the day, he asked himself: "What good have I done today?"

Franklin kept to this plan for most of his life. He commented: "It is the more remarkable, as being formed when I was so young, and yet being pretty faithfully adhered to quite thro' old age."

Benevolence

As human beings, we all need each other. When we are benevolent towards others, we may not immediately benefit. But benevolence is not about expecting benefits — we extend it from the goodness of our hearts. Directly or indirectly, that kindness will come back to us. This virtue seems the least related to studies and examinations. Still, it can play an important part.

When I was doing my master's degree course, I had a graphic artist in my office who was a "problem worker". He frequently turned up late for work and often took leave to attend to his personal matters, until he had no leave entitlement left.

I allowed him unrecorded time off to settle his personal affairs, on the condition that if work demands required him to stay back late, he would do so. I was taking a big risk in helping him. If my boss found out that I had given him unrecorded time off, I would be punished.

Besides helping him, I commended him whenever he produced good work. Soon, the graphic artist turned into a model worker. He consistently reported early for work and the quality of his work was superb. He also became very loyal and helpful towards me. Thus, I was freed from the stress of having to deal with a problem worker at the office. I could now focus my attention on my own work.

My most significant experience of benevolence was when I was at the receiving end of it, from my pre-university college mate, Diana. Even though we were not close friends in the beginning, Diana sensed that I was troubled and asked me if I needed to talk. She gave me a much needed listening ear. More than that, she coached me in Mathematics everyday during the school vacation. Except on the day I passed, she would never allow me to buy her a meal to show my appreciation, because she knew I came from a poor family. This was true benevolence on her part. I had done nothing to deserve the tremendous help that she gave me.

The Good Samaritan

Probably the most famous story about benevolence is that of the Good Samaritan, as told by Jesus in the Bible. According to the story, a Jew was travelling along

(*Continued*)

(*Continued*)

a highway one day when he was robbed, beaten and left to die. A Jewish priest and a Levite (assistant priest) passed by, but they crossed to the other side to avoid the man. Then came a Samaritan (person from Samaria). The Samaritans were traditional enemies of the Jews. In spite of this, the Samaritan stopped to help the Jew. He dressed his wounds, took him to an inn, left some money for the innkeeper to take care of the man, and continued his journey. He further told the innkeeper that he would drop by on his way back and make up for any shortfall if needed.

This story has since become so famous that, more than two thousand years after the story was first told, people who perform extraordinary charitable deeds are called "Samaritans".

Was the Samaritan extraordinary? Not really. In fact, he was so ordinary that nobody knows his name. The only thing that made him special was that he cared for someone else when that person was in need. This is true benevolence.

Strategy

"Strategy without tactics is the slowest route to victory. Tactics without strategy is the noise before defeat."

— *Sun Zi*, The Art of War

Strategy involves doing things in a deliberate way that is calculated to produce certain results. With the correct strategy, you can win even if you are in a weaker position.

As an example, a king once challenged his rival to a horse racing contest, knowing full well that his horses were superior. The rival thought about it and proposed three races. The one who won at least two would win the contest. The king readily agreed. In the first race, the king fielded his best horse. His rival fielded his worst horse. So the rival lost. In the second race, the king could only field his second best horse. The rival fielded his best, and won. By now, you can guess who won the third race, and the contest!

The greatest difference between my old and new approaches to studies was that, when I did my postgraduate studies, I had a strategy. Previously, some of the things I did in school or even at university, such as trying to spot questions, I thought were part of my "strategy". But they were not — I was merely doing them out of desperation.

Without a strategy, some of the things I did haphazardly were:

- taking notes in a disorganised manner — my notes were useless when I needed to revise for my examinations;
- not revising until the last minute, usually only a few days before the examinations;
- having a negative view of examinations;
- answering my exam questions hurriedly, without reading the questions and instructions carefully;

- memorising rather than seeking to understand the subject matter;
- never evaluating where I had gone wrong or how I could have done better after the examinations.

The PRAISE model is influenced by Sun Zi's *The Art of War,* which is one of the greatest books on strategy ever written. PRAISE gives a broad sweep of the process of planning and implementing a strategy through a five-step process called FREED, which stands for:

- ***F***oundation
- ***R***evision
- ***E***xamination
- ***E***valuation
- ***D***iscipline

These five elements of strategy form a continuous process of learning. Each episode in life contains lessons that prepare us for the next. Strategy equips us with a lifelong **LEARNING** formula.

Jollibee vs McDonald's

Philippine fast food company Jollibee took on fast food giant McDonald's — and won, thanks to their strategy.

(*Continued*)

(*Continued*)

Jollibee was established by Filipino entrepreneur Tony Tan, who started off in 1975 with two ice-cream parlours. Inspired by the global success of McDonald's, Tan opened his own chain of seven hamburger restaurants called Jollibee in 1978.

In 1979, he and his brothers travelled to the US to observe every detail about how McDonald's operated. They returned and remodelled their stores exactly like McDonald's, except that Jollibee kept to its own menu, with foods catered to Philippine taste buds.

In 1981, McDonald's opened in the Philippines. However, Jollibee had already become firmly entrenched as the market leader. Not only was McDonald's unable to unseat it, the fast food giant did so badly that *The Economist* reported in 2002: "The Philippines is a huge embarrassment to McDonald's." Currently, in the Philippines, Jollibee controls about two-thirds of the market, where McDonald's is a distant second.

Foundation

"If I had eight hours to chop down a tree, I'd spend six sharpening my ax."

— ***Abraham Lincoln, former US President***

This book is intended to lay your foundation in terms of a positive attitude towards studies, as a strong foundation improves the chances of victory or success. While many books have been written about study and examination techniques, these techniques are merely tools. If a person is not motivated, even the best tools will not produce anything.

When a person is motivated, he or she will seek out the best tools and exploit them to the fullest. Even if the person does not have the best tools, he or she will make the best use of whatever is available. So even though tools can be helpful, what really matters is the person using them.

If you are studying for an examination, you obviously need to understand the subject well. That is your foundation. Many students practise answering questions from previous years' examinations and this practice adds to their foundation.

It also helps if you rest well the night before so that you enter the examination hall with a mind that is fresh and clear. Foundation has many aspects. The more thorough you are, the more aspects you will cover, and the stronger your foundation will be.

In my postgraduate studies, I adopted a different attitude towards examinations. I viewed the examination as an opportunity for me to demonstrate my knowledge, not as a trap to expose my ignorance. This change in attitude laid my foundation at a very deep level. Without the right mental attitude, I would probably not have done as well as I did.

Thomas Edison is widely regarded as a genius, yet some medical experts have speculated that he had learning difficulties, for he was strangely weak in areas such as cognition, speech and grammar. He had little formal education and was largely taught at home by his mother. But he read widely and, at one stage, planned to read every book on his father's bookshelf.

Another important foundation for Edison was his knack for entrepreneurship. At age 12, Edison sold newspapers, snacks and candy on the railroad. He also employed other children to sell fruits and vegetables. At 14, he published his own newspaper. It was the first newspaper ever to be typeset, printed and sold on a train. At one time, he was earning more than $10 per day, which was a large sum of money back then. This business spirit was important because Edison was able to produce practical inventions and commercialise them.

Edison also suffered from hearing loss. He turned this setback to his advantage and used the silence associated with deafness to enhance his concentration.

Edison's most significant foundation, however, was his learning of Morse code and the telegraph at age 15. He had saved a toddler from being knocked down by a runaway freight car on the railway tracks and, as a reward, the boy's father taught him the use of the

(*Continued*)

(*Continued*)

telegraph. Born in 1847, Edison grew up during the Age of Telegraphy and the use of the telegraph was a very valuable skill then.

Revision

In the context of strategy, revision refers to the act of altering and modifying one's strategy.

In terms of revising for my examinations, I certainly had to change my strategy. In school and at university, I treated revision as a last minute task to refresh my memory just before my examinations. Later, I realised that examinations were not about memorising but about understanding. If I already had a good understanding, there would be no need for any revision. I could sit for an examination at any time and do well in it.

To prepare for my examinations, I wrote out a revision plan, allocating time for practising past questions and project work, as well as for social and leisure activities in order to maintain a healthy balance. Because I had done my revisions regularly throughout the school year, the process was effortless and painless. It was very different from the intense and stressful last minute revision that I did previously.

Canon, Inc.

Canon, the highly successful camera maker, went through constant management changes during its early years in the 1930s and 1940s. The original founder of the company left the business after less than a year. His partner was posted to Singapore during the Second World War and he left the running of the business to his friend, Takeshi Mitarai, who proved more capable than he and later took control over the company.

The name of the camera was changed from *Kwanon* (the Japanese name for the Buddhist Goddess of Mercy) to Canon. The company name was changed from *Seiki Kogaku Kenyisho* (SKK) to Canon Camera Co. Inc., and the writing of the company's name was changed from Japanese characters to the romanised alphabet. Slowly, Canon evolved towards becoming an international company.

Another major revision came in August 1945, when Takeshi Mitarai wound up the company and started afresh two months later, hiring only those employees who were loyal during the war.

Probably the most major revision came in 1975, the year Canon made a loss of about $5.7 million and

(*Continued*)

(*Continued*)

could not pay dividends to its shareholders. Major management reforms were instituted. Canon pursued a path of diversification and quickly returned to profitability.

These and other changes helped Canon become the US$35 billion company that it was in 2006.

Examination

Examination in the context of strategy goes beyond examinations associated with studying. It refers to putting one's plan to the test, in order to gauge the results. It could mean a trial run or mock examination, whereby the student practises past questions. Of course, it also includes an actual examination where students' marks are graded.

For my individual presentations in the master's degree programme, I did trial runs before a few classmates who were kind enough to spare the time. I took their feedback seriously and worked on improving my presentation before I presented it to the entire class. Without practice, my first individual presentation turned out to be a disaster. But I learnt a lot from that incident. I appreciated the importance of doing trial runs and subsequently fared much better.

Dare to Fail

Tom Peters, co-author of *In Search of Excellence*, once asked David Glass, at that time CEO of WalMart, the largest retailer in the world, how he would describe Walmart founder Sam Walton. Glass replied: "Sam is not afraid to fail. Sam will try something and he will make a horrible botch of it; then he will walk in to work the next morning, laughing like a hyena, and he would say, 'Got that one out of the way. What the hell do we do next?' "

Evaluation

In the past, whenever I did badly in my studies, I simply accepted my poor results. I felt that there was nothing I could do about it. PRAISE taught me to evaluate my performance — and to do something about it!

In my diploma course, I obtained a B for my first paper. I wanted to be a top student and I knew that B's would not get me to the top. So I conducted an evaluation to discover my mistakes and weak areas and how I could overcome them in the future.

Some of the areas I considered in my evaluation were:

- Was I adversely influenced by SADDLE factors — self-pity, arrogance, distractions, daydreams, laziness, exaggerated fear?

- Did I have any problem with time management?
- Was I adequate in note-making and in producing mind maps?
- Did I have any poor study habits?
- Did I have sufficient course material?
- Was my foundation strong enough?
- Were there gaps in my revision plan?
- Were there weaknesses in the way I approached the exam?

By making a thorough evaluation of my performance, I was able to perform much better subsequently.

A "Happy Problem"

Urgent evaluation is obviously needed when a project goes horribly wrong. Bul what if things go "horribly right"?

This was what happened to **Sakae Sushi,** a conveyor-belt sushi restaurant started by Singapore entrepreneur Douglas Foo. When Foo opened his first Sakae Sushi restaurant in September 1977, he ran out of food within three hours.

Such a "happy problem", if not solved, will turn into an unhappy one. If Sakae Sushi had kept running out of food, it would not likely have become the success it is today — as Singapore's biggest chain of sushi restaurants, with branches in Indonesia, Thailand and China.

Discipline

There are two types of discipline — internal and external. Internal discipline is self-imposed and more effective. External discipline is imposed by a higher authority. It may not be as effective because once the authority is not around, the discipline may evaporate.

For any project to be successful — and even for daily routines to proceed smoothly — the people involved need to observe internal as well as external "system" discipline.

System discipline also requires that the interest of the group be placed above personal interest. When I had a disagreement with my team members over the source of motivation, I went along with the majority view for the group presentation. I presented my own view only when I wrote about my individual learning experience.

The situation was different when I had a dispute with my team leader over my clarification of the word "exercises". If I had not clarified, I would not have been able to contribute meaningfully to the group discussion. So I persisted. Should I have backed off to avoid a conflict? No. If I did that, I might have felt bitter and any negative feeling on my part could have rubbed off onto the other team members.

There are no hard and fast rules. Sometimes it is better to have a short-term flare-up and then move on. At other times, it may be best to avoid an open confrontation. Perhaps the only rule I can offer is to think about what is best for the whole group, and act accordingly.

The greatest challenge for me was doing the master's course itself. The first year was especially difficult as I was concurrently doing my diploma programme and holding a full-time job. Many times, I wanted to give up. In the end, though, discipline saw me through.

Downing of Korean Aircraft

In 1983, a Korean aircraft veered into Soviet airspace. According to later investigation, this was due to navigation equipment failure. But the aircraft did not have navigation lights on, and its pilots did not respond to communication messages from the Soviets.

As a result, it was shot down as Soviet military officers thought it was an enemy aircraft. There were no good guys and bad guys in this tragedy. Unfortunately, the Korean aircraft had failed to observe system discipline.

Excellence

"He can who thinks he can, he can't who thinks he can't."

— Pablo Piccaso, artist

"Think you can, think you can't, either way you'll be right."

— Henry Ford, industrialist

Success — and failure — begins in the mind. With mind power, you can do all sorts of fantastic things — climb mountains, run marathons, lose weight, recover from illness . . . and pass your exams with flying colours.

What are the chances of success if you set out to do something, even if it is something you have never done before? The answer may surprise you. According to research by psychoanalyst Karen Horney, people who embark on new tasks succeed 95 percent of the time!

The trouble is, most people do not even try and they think they failed. But this failure is not real. How can you fail at something that you did not do?

Power of Positive Thinking

Normal Vincent Peale (1898–1993) popularised the idea of positive thinking. His 1952 book, *The Power of Positive Thinking*, was on the New York Times bestseller list for 186 consecutive weeks. It sold over 20 million copies and has been translated into more than 40 languages.

Peale grew up with a strong inferiority complex and was "shy to the extreme". He was so lacking in confidence that his college professor once told him: "You have a reasonably good mind but you are not making

(*Continued*)

(*Continued*)

adequate use of it. How long are you going to be like this — a scared rabbit afraid of establishing its own voice? You better change the way you think about yourself. You better do it now before it's too late!"

Peale later found a book by the 19th-century psychologist William James, who wrote: "The greatest discovery of this generation is that a human being can alter his life by altering his attitudes of mind."

Peale went on to make himself confident by acting confident, and talking about it. Interestingly, he owes the success of *The Power of Positive Thinking* to the positive attitude of his wife. Peale received so many rejection slips for his book that he threw the manuscript into the waste basket and forbade his wife from removing it. The next day, his wife took the entire waste basket to another publisher, who finally accepted it!

Pygmalion effect

In some instances, such as in teacher-student relationships, even how other people think of you can affect your performance. If they believe you will do well, chances are you will. And if they think you will do badly, chances are you also will. This is the Pygmalion Effect, named after a book, *Pygmalion in the Classroom*, by Robert Rosenthal, a professor of social psychology, and Lenore Jacobson.

In a 1968 study, the two Harvard researchers made a group of students sit for an IQ test and then told teachers that 20 percent of them showed great potential for intellectual development. In reality, the students were chosen randomly. But because their teachers were led to believe that they were intellectually superior, these students significantly improved their scores when they sat for a second IQ test eight months later.

What can you do about the Pygmalion Effect? First, try your best to create a positive image of yourself. If you cannot show that you are smart, at least show that you are sincere about wanting to learn.

Second, avoid a negative image. Do not misbehave or sleep in class, do not hand in your assignments late and so on. Otherwise, you will need to work doubly hard to change your teachers' view of you.

Self-talk

Our mind can be considered a "separate person" and we often talk to ourselves. Most of us do it silently, but some people do it aloud and are considered "mad". Yet, it is very natural to talk to ourselves.

What do you talk to yourself about? What do you keep telling yourself, day after day?

Some people tell themselves that they are bad with numbers, or bad at remembering facts. This is their "self-talk". For most people, self-talk tends to be negative. For some, it can get really bad, like "I can never succeed at anything" or "I always fail no matter how hard I try."

If you have a lot of negative self-talk, you need to change this. Start with small changes. Instead of saying "I can never succeed", change it to "I can succeed if I set a lower target" or "I can find someone to help me."

And why not? If some people can get 100 marks for Mathematics, why can't you get 70 or 80? If some people can learn six languages, why can't you learn two? If some students can score 10 A's, why can't you score at least 10 B's? Why must you fail?

Cycles of excellence

"We are what we repeatedly do. Excellence, then, is not an act but a habit."

— Aristotle, Greek philosopher

"He that is good for making excuses is seldom good for anything else."

— Benjamin Franklin, scientist, inventor, statesman

"I am not a has been. I am a will be."

— Lauren Bacall, actress

Once you have achieved excellence, you want to do it over and over again — not because you are greedy for success, but because you have to. Otherwise, you will stagnate and deteriorate.

Some people achieve success at an early age, but then something happens and they fall, never to rise again. So it is important that when you experience a setback, you are able to pick yourself up and move on to greater heights.

A person who fails to pick himself up lacks resilience. He may be gifted with intelligence or born into a favourable family environment. But because he never created his own success, he will not know how to reproduce it once he fails.

When we learn to reproduce excellence and success, over and over again, we become a successful person — a person with a clear pattern of success all the time. We therefore acquire a lifetime **Excellence** formula.

Life is a continuous process of study and examination. Even after you leave school, you will always keep learning new things. It could be something minor. Let's say you bought a new digital camera or some other gadget. Can you learn to use all or most of its functions? This may seem trivial. But some people have mental blocks that prevent them from learning even simple tasks.

In the course of your work, you may also have to undertake major learning projects, such as studying the feasibility of launching a new product or expanding to new markets. Can you pass these "examinations"? Or if you fail, can you rebound from the setback?

PRAISE is specially designed to help you overcome setbacks and achieve excellence, over and over again. You will enter a cycle whereby success breeds greater success. This cycle has five elements:

- Action
- Success
- Habit
- Character
- Perseverance

Action

Action can lead to either success or failure. If failure occurs, you go back to taking action again. If you keep failing, obviously your action is not appropriate and you need to take some other form of action.

If you keep failing your examinations, what should you do? Keep studying (or not studying) in the same way? This is not going to work.

You need to discover what forms of action give you the best results. Be flexible in your approach. In fact, start by thinking differently. You need to change your attitudes before you even change your actions.

Action also means going though the SUCCESS 6 Formula:

- ***S***et the ***P***rizedream
- ***U***se internal ***R***ules
- ***C***onduct ***A***nalysis

- ***C***ultivate ***I***nvincibility
- ***E***xecute the ***S***trategy
- ***S***ustain ***E***xcellence
- ***S***uccess shall be yours, without limits.

If your action does not lead to success, go back to the first steps of the PRAISE model to examine where you have gone wrong and where improvements can be made. If you apply the SUCCESS 6 Formula diligently, you should meet with success soon enough.

Success

Once you have achieved success, you will have attained a new level of life skills. You will have broken free from your past patterns of failure, mediocrity or, at best, "lucky success".

"Lucky success" — coming from favourable circumstances — is not true success. It cannot be repeated because nobody is always lucky. Some people may appear always lucky. But if you look deeper, you will find that they had their share of setbacks, and that they worked hard to take full advantage of whatever "luck" they had.

If you depend on "luck", you may not be able to bounce back once a setback occurs. But once you have learnt how to create your own success, all setbacks become temporary. They become part of the learning experience that will lead you to greater successes.

Small Successes

Do One Thing Different is a book by psychotherapist Bill O'Hanlon, who is a great believer that small changes can lead to big successes. A favourite anecdote of his is about how one woman overcame her drug addiction by making just one very small change.

In 1999, Bill appeared on the popular *Oprah Winfrey Show*. A woman who watched the show e-mailed Bill and asked him to recommend psychotherapists who used similar approaches as he. Bill gave her three names, but never heard from her again.

A year later, Bill finally received another e-mail from the woman. She had contacted all the three psychotherapists, but could not afford their fees. So she decided to heal herself of the addiction by doing "one thing different".

She was taking 27 pills a day. Her addiction was so strong that even to reduce her intake by one pill was too big a step for her. She finally came up with a plan to scrape a bit off each pill.

That was the one small change. As the weeks passed, she would scrape off more and more of it. Ten months later, she had scraped so much off that she was no longer taking the drug.

(*Continued*)

(*Continued*)

This first step to success was important. It boosted her confidence and made her believe that she could eventually achieve bigger successes.

Habit

Once you are able to achieve success, no matter how small, the next step is to make a habit of it. Keep striving for success so that you are constantly, habitually successful.

The fact that you succeed is more important than the size of your success. So if you are not yet very capable, set modest targets. It is better to achieve minor successes most of the time, than to achieve big successes occasionally but fail the rest of the time.

At pre-university, I would sleep at 7 p.m. and wake up at 2 a.m. to study. This was very difficult at first. But as I made it a habit, it became easier. Waking up at 2 a.m. became more of a daily routine, rather than something that required special effort.

Franklin's Habits

When Benjamin Franklin drew up his list of virtues, he originally had only 12, but he added "humility" as the

(*Continued*)

(Continued)

13th virtue after a friend pointed out that he was generally thought to be proud.

Franklin was determined to cure himself of this vice or folly, so he adopted a new strategy in his manner of speaking: "I even forbid myself . . . the use of every word or expression in the language that imported a fix'd opinion, such as certainly, undoubtedly, etc., and I adopted, instead of them, I conceive, I apprehend, or I imagine a thing to be so or so; or it so appears to me at present."

Naturally, Franklin found it difficult when he first tried to change. But he soon made a habit of it: ". . . it became at length so easy, and so habitual to me, that perhaps for these fifty years past no one has ever heard a dogmatical expression escape me."

Franklin believed this habit helped him to sway public opinion: ". . . for I was but a bad speaker, never eloquent, subject to much hesitation in my choice of words, hardly correct in language, and yet I generally carried my points."

Character

At university, my habit of helping some of the weaker students, and of improving my grades year after year, soon became part of my character. I acquired a reputation of being a "good student".

This was a vast improvement from before. In primary school, my character was that of a playful, naughty failure. Up until pre-university, the best I could manage was to become a "barely made it" student.

The reputation I acquired at university, however, came to nought when I joined the master's degree programme. This was a programme for mid-career adults and most of my classmates held high positions in their organisations. In contrast, I was a young naval officer with zero corporate experience.

I was considered a nobody. My classmates did not want me for group projects as they worried I would drag down the overall score. Thus, I had to re-establish my character — by achieving success and making a habit of it.

I consciously made it a habit to volunteer to take notes during our group discussions and produce the final report. I put my heart and soul into the task so that I consistently produced good reports. As the course progressed, I also stopped asking basic questions in class and began contributing more meaningfully towards class discussions.

Slowly, as I established my character as a helpful and capable student, my classmates began to see me for my value. I began to be invited by various groups to join them in their projects.

British billionaire entrepreneur **Richard Branson** has such a strong success character that few people know, and care, about his failures.

Some years back, Branson opened his Virgin megastore and launched his Virgin soft drinks in Singapore. Both projects failed.

Branson probably had other failed ventures as well. Do they matter? I don't think so. His successes with Virgin Atlantic, Virgin Blue and other businesses have been immense. So what if he occasionally failed?

That is the great advantage of being successful — you can afford to fail. You can make mistakes, shrug them off and learn from them. You can even afford to do things that you know little about. One of Branson's latest business ventures is space tourism. Of this, he said: "I couldn't change a spark plug and I started Virgin Atlantic. And I haven't got a clue about spaceships."

If you adopt the mindset of a failure, one mistake can devastate you and even drive you to depression. But if you have the character of a success, even a hundred mistakes will not matter. You can take on the toughest challenges and not worry too much about failing.

A message we often hear is that in order to succeed, one must not be afraid of failure. This is true. But it is a chicken and egg situation — in order not to be afraid of failure, you have to succeed first.

How can you break free from this situation? Begin by starting small. Take small risks and achieve small successes. Build your confidence. From there, slowly make success a habit. Finally, when that habit becomes a part of your character, you will feel so confident about yourself that failures will not bother you anymore.

Perseverance

Once you have made success a habit and acquired the character of a successful person, the next step is relatively easy — persevere.

Perseverance means that you keep applying the PRAISE SUCCESS 6 Formula to achieve round after round of success. It also means that you guard against complacency so that you do not slacken. This is something that happens all too easily.

My master's degree course culminated in a "consolidated examination" that tested students' knowledge and familiarity with all the subjects taught in the 11 previous modules. This was the ultimate test. We not only had to be familiar with all the subjects, but also with how they inter-related with one another.

I prepared well for it right from the start. In my ongoing note-making and revision for each of the modules, I was already integrating my notes by incorporating concepts from one module into another. I was already laying the foundation for this final paper.

For an examination such as this, it was impossible to study from textbooks as they did not cover how the different subjects were inter-related. Moreover, this examination required us to draw from our presentations, group projects and class discussions.

Most importantly, having persevered to do well in every module, I felt mentally prepared to tackle the consolidated examination. There was no single subject that I was weak in. I could easily draw knowledge and insights from one situation to apply in another.

And so I passed, with flying colours. My PRAISE life skills model passed as well, also with flying colours.

The PRAISE model played a crucial role in helping me achieve my Prizedream. I did not realise it then, but I was to achieve many more Prizedreams when I ventured into the corporate world and the world of entrepreneurship.

There are still other Prizedreams yet to be achieved. My days of "Prizedreaming" have only just begun . . .

Be Careful

Be careful of your thoughts,
for your thoughts become your words;

Be careful of your words,
for your words become your deeds;

Be careful of your deeds,
for your deeds become your habits;

Be careful of your habits,
for your habits become your character;

Be careful of your character,
for your character becomes your destiny.

— **Anonymous**

inspire

Part II

LIFE SKILLS

inspire

5

∞ Success Unlimited

Studies and examinations are important, but they are not as crucial as the life skills that you acquire in the process of getting good grades. As will be seen in the next chapter, people with a good set of life skills can succeed — and succeed in fantastic ways — even though they might not have much formed education.

After I topped my master's degree course, I went on to apply the PRAISE life skills model in my corporate career, entrepreneurship and other life's challenges. I have now been using PRAISE for over 20 years and it has never failed me.

PRAISE can be applied to a broad range of situations because all challenges are basically the same — they all require you to overcome obstacles, rebound from setbacks and never give up.

With a good set of life skills, therefore, you will be able to achieve success in many different fields and in many different aspects of your life, making you a truly successful person.

If you are a top student but you don't know how to socialise, your classmates will call you a nerd. If you succeed in making a lot of money but fail to manage your finances, you are a failure. If you build a business empire but you have no family or friends, you have failed in life. If you are well-respected in your organisation but your own children do not respect you, something is obviously amiss.

Life has many facets and we may not succeed in every single aspect of it. We must, nevertheless, strive for success in as many areas as possible. Even in those areas where we don't quite succeed, at least we can work towards reducing the extent of our failures.

People who succeed strongly in one area tend to do so at the expense of other aspects of their lives. They may leave great imprints on humanity, but their personal lives suffer.

As Chief Executive Officer and Chairman of KPMG, one of the largest accounting firms in the US, **Eugene O'Kelly** had power and prestige. He felt that he "sat atop the world". That perspective changed when, in May 2005 at age 53, O'Kelly was diagnosed with brain cancer. He was told that he might not live beyond September.

(*Continued*)

(Continued)

He wrote: "But the job of CEO, while of course incredibly privileged, was relentless. My diary was perpetually extended out over the next 18 months. I worked weekends and late into many nights. I missed virtually every school function for my younger daughter. Over the course of my last decade with the firm, I did manage to squeeze in work-day lunches with my wife. Twice . . ."

Re-evaluating his success, O'Kelly lived his final days spending more time with his family and writing about his final days. On 10 September 2005, O'Kelly died. His wife Corinne wrote the final chapter of his book, *Chasing Daylight: How My Forthcoming Death Transformed My Life.*

It is not uncommon that the prospect of death makes people re-evaluate what they want out of life. In the process, they often strike a new balance and redefine the meaning of "success".

We all need to find our own balance. I therefore encourage you to define your own success and choose the type of success that you want. Choose to be successful according to your own definition — and act on it.

Success, as defined by others, will understandably influence us, due to social norms, peer pressure and other reasons. So, yes, it is not easy to find your own definition of success. Nevertheless, you must make your choice and take ownership of it, so that you become master of your own destiny.

6

Famous Failures

Stories abound about how geniuses like Albert Einstein and highly successful entrepreneurs like Bill Gates were failures and dropouts.

Some of these stories are not entirely accurate. True, Bill Gates did not complete his university education. But he left during his third year to pursue a career in computer software development and to start a business with his friend — a business that eventually became Microsoft Corporation. His decision to leave was not because he could not cope with his studies.

Bill Gates had left Harvard University, which is widely considered to be the top university in the world! He was reported to have gained admission to Harvard with a SAT (Scholastic Assessment Test) score of 1590 — a score that would have placed him among the top 0.1 percent of candidates. He was not the regular "college dropout".

In the same "class" as Bill Gates is Michael Dell, founder of Dell Computers. He did not do well in school and one of his teachers had commented that he "would probably never go anywhere in life".

While at the University of Texas at Austin studying to become a doctor, Dell started a computer company called PC's Limited. The company did so well that, at the age of 19, Dell stopped his studies to run the business full-time.

Today, PC's Limited has become Dell Computer Corporation, the largest personal computer manufacturer in the world. And Michael Dell was ranked by *Forbes Magazine* in 2006 as the 12th richest man in the world.

The case of Albert Einstein (1879–1955) is a bit more complicated. His "failure" in mathematics was, in fact, due to a confusion caused by a change in the way grades were assigned.

Einstein was not weak in mathematics. He actually showed an aptitude for mathematics at an early age. Einstein attended the Luitpold Gymnasium, a secondary school in Munich, Germany, and he began to learn mathematics when he was about 12 years old. He taught himself Euclidean plane geometry from a school booklet and also began to study calculus.

He was, however, considered a "slow learner". This could have been due to dyslexia, a learning disorder whereby sufferers have difficulty recognising alphabets and words. It could also have been due simply to shyness. But later in life,

Einstein credited his development of the theory of relativity to this slowness, saying that by pondering space and time later than most children, he was able to apply a more developed intellect.

In 1894, following the failure of his father's electrochemical business, the Einsteins moved from Munich to Pavia, a city in Italy. Einstein remained behind in Munich to finish school, but he completed only one term before leaving to join his family in Pavia. Einstein quit school — by obtaining a medical note from a friendly doctor — a year and a half before the final examinations. Thus, he did not have a secondary-school certificate.

Einstein took the entrance examination of the *Eidgenössische Technische Hochschule* (Swiss Federal Institute of Technology) and excelled in science and mathematics. However, he failed the liberal arts portion of the exam. His family sent him to Aarau, Switzerland, to finish secondary school. There, he studied electromagnetic theory and received his diploma in September 1896.

So, whether or not Einstein was in fact a "slow learner", he still went on to become arguably the greatest scientist of the 20th century; the icon of genius and intelligence!

Albert Einstein, Bill Gates and Michael Dell are the more famous examples of "successful dropouts", even though they were not dropouts in the true sense of the word. There are many more, including those who did badly in school as well as those who dropped out for other reasons. How many?

One website that lists "Noted High School and Elementary School Dropouts" counted 699 as of February 2006.

Many of the people on the list are movie stars and pop or rock singers. They include 63 Oscar winners, 103 Oscar nominees and uncounted numbers of other award winners. Sports personalities also featured prominently on the list, including 7 Olympic gold medalists.

Significantly, the list of "famous dropouts" also includes:

- 18 billionaires and uncounted numbers of millionaires
- 8 US Presidents and several other world leaders
- 10 Nobel Prize winners (6 Literature, 2 Peace, 1 Physics, 1 Chemistry)
- 55 bestselling authors
- 27 knighthoods and 3 damehoods.

Yet this impressive list includes mainly people who are well-known within the English-speaking world. In Europe, Asia and elsewhere, I am sure there are lots more successful dropouts.

For instance, Li Ka Shing, the richest man in Asia, is one famous billionaire not (yet) on this list. In China, so I was told but could not verify, the majority of the country's richest and most successful entrepreneurs are people with minimal education.

It has to be noted that "dropouts" in this case refer to people who left the education system for a variety of reasons, not necessarily due to a lack of academic ability. Some were too poor to continue their studies, some stopped schooling because of war, family dislocation, poor health, and other reasons.

Thus, the list also includes a number of people who subsequently obtained at least the equivalent of a high school diploma, as well as degrees and doctorates. But they form a minority — 138 out of 699 people, or about 20 percent. The rest never made it past high school. But they made it in life!

The compilers of the list write:

> *"While it is a fact and very important to stress that more opportunities exist for individuals who have at least a high school diploma, the names on these lists also add considerable weight to the discussion of what constitutes markers of human intelligence and a person's potential worth to society and, historically, civilization as a whole.*
>
> *These names represent examples of human perseverance, creativity, and, in a great many instances, genius."*

The following pages feature just a few examples . . .

"Colonel" Harland Sanders (1890–1980)

Colonel Sanders is the founder of Kentucky Fried Chicken (KFC), one of the biggest fast food chains in the world today. He dropped out of elementary school in his fifth year, but later earned a law degree through a correspondence course.

Sanders' father died when he was six years old, and he had to cook for the family as his mother worked. He worked on many jobs during his teenage years, including firefighter, steamboat driver, insurance salesman and as a private in the Cuban army.

At the age of 40, he ran a service station in Corbin, Kentucky, and cooked chicken for people who passed by. His popularity grew and he moved to a motel and restaurant and began working as the chef.

But not all was well. In 1952, Sanders was in his 60s and reportedly penniless. He travelled across the US to licence his special method of frying chicken in a pressure cooker, sleeping in his car to save money. His proposal was that restaurant owners would pay him a nickel (five cents) for every piece of chicken sold.

Over a two-year period, he was rejected 1,008 times before the 1,009th person said "Yes". And so KFC was born.

José Saramago (1922–)

Saramago is a Portuguese writer who won the Nobel Prize for Literature in 1998. He dropped out of grammar school due to his family's financial situation and later attended a technical school where he received training to become a car mechanic.

In his autobiography, Saramago wrote:

"I was born into a family of landless peasants . . . I was a good pupil at primary school: in the second class I was writing with no spelling mistakes and the third and fourth classes were done in a single year. Then I was moved up to the grammar school where I stayed two years, with excellent marks in the first year, not so good in the second, but was well-liked by classmates and teachers.

Meanwhile my parents reached the conclusion that, in the absence of resources, they could not go on keeping me in the grammar school. The only alternative for me was to go to a technical school. And so it was: for five years, I learned to be a mechanic. But surprisingly, the syllabus at that time, though obviously technically-oriented, included, besides French, a literature subject.

After finishing the course, I worked for two years as a mechanic at a car repair shop. By that time I had already started to frequent, in its evening opening hours, a public library in Lisbon. And it was there, with no help or guidance except curiosity and the will to learn, that my taste for reading developed and was refined."

Arnold Schwarzenegger (1947–)

Schwarzenegger left school at 14 to focus on bodybuilding and to work as an apprentice carpenter. He became one of the world's greatest bodybuilders, a successful actor and film producer and, since November 2003, the Governor of California, USA.

Born in Austria, Schwarzenegger played many sports as a child and discovered his passion for bodybuilding when, during his teens, his soccer coach took the team for weight training.

At 18, Schwarzenegger served in the Austrian army. One day, he sneaked off from the army base to compete in his first bodybuilding competition. He won the junior title of Mr Australasia. He was punished for sneaking off, but reportedly earned the respect of his army superiors.

In September 1968, Schwarzenegger moved to the United States. He had little money and limited knowledge of English. But he had a dream — to become the greatest bodybuilder in the world by winning the prestigious Mr Olympia contest.

He failed in his first attempt in 1969, but won for the next six consecutive years, from 1970 to 1975. In 1980, as a late entry with only eight weeks to prepare for the competition, Schwarzenegger again won the Mr Olympia title.

Meanwhile, Schwarzenegger embarked on a successful Hollywood career and is best known for the movies, *Terminator* and *Terminator II: Judgement Day.*

Lesser known about Schwarzenegger is that he became a millionaire at age 22, before his bodybuilding and Hollywood successes. He made his money through a brick-laying business which he co-founded with another bodybuilder in 1968. The duo later started a mail order business for bodybuilding equipment and instructional tapes and Schwarzenegger also invested in real estate.

In addition, Schwarzenegger was a founding "celebrity investor" in the Planet Hollywood chain of theme restaurants, launched in 1991. He severed his ties with the business in 2000.

In 2003, Schwarzenegger was elected Governor of California. Along his career path, as a 32-year-old adult in 1979, he graduated from the University of Wisconsin-Superior with degrees in International Marketing of Fitness and Business Administration.

Wally Amos (1936–)

Wally Amos is the founder of the Famous Amos international chain of cookie stores and, more recently, Uncle Wally's Muffin Company.

Amos had little formal education, but showed interest in cooking from a very young age. He enrolled at the Food Trades Vocational High School, but dropped out to join the US Air Force.

Whilst in the Air Force, Amos became inspired to study. He obtained a high school diploma and, after leaving the Air Force, went to college to study to become a secretary. He took on a clerical job with William Morris Agency, where he worked with pop stars including Diana Ross & the Supremes and Simon & Garfunkel.

Amos attracted clients to the William Morris Agency by sending them an invitation along with some chocolate chip cookies that he baked, using his aunt's recipe which he learnt as a child.

In 1975, a friend encouraged him to set up a cookie store and the first Famous Amos store was opened in Los Angeles. Later, financial troubles forced Amos to sell his company, but he made a comeback with The Uncle Noname's Cookie Company.

A Famous Amos distributor, Lou Avignone, heard Amos on a local radio talk show and was inspired by his early business success and his indomitable spirit. Avignone contacted Amos and, in 1994, the two launched a new business called Uncle Noname Gourmet Muffins, producing fat-free, nutritious muffins. In 1999, Uncle Noname became Uncle Wally's Muffin Company.

Today, Amos has become a motivational speaker and is author of 13 books, including *Watermelon Magic: Seeds of Wisdom, Slices of Life*, and *The Famous Amos Story: The Face That Launched a Thousand Chips.*

James H. Clark (1944–)

Clark was suspended from high school for misbehaviour, but went on to earn a PhD in computer science — and revolutionise computer and the Internet technology.

He is the father of computer graphics and, as co-founder of Netscape Communications, a pioneer of Internet web surfing. He also sparked the dot.com boom on the US stock market during the 1990s, and is widely considered a genius.

Clark had a difficult childhood. His father was reportedly an alcoholic and a wife abuser, and his parents divorced when he was about 14. Clark and his brother were supported by their mother on a meagre salary and Clark severed ties with his father.

At high school, Clark once smuggled a skunk into a school dance. And when an English teacher scolded him for failing to read a poem, *The Rime of the Ancient Mariner*, Clark told her to go to hell. He was suspended for setting off a smoke bomb on the band bus.

Clark eventually joined the Navy. After nine months at sea, he took a Mathematics test and scored the highest marks. He returned to studying, earned bachelor's and master's degrees in Physics and a doctorate in Computer Science, and became a university professor.

Clark's research enabled computers to display graphics quickly. He founded Silicon Graphics and the company become a world leader in movie special effects, such as those seen in *Star Wars*.

In 1994, after falling out with Silicon Graphics, Clark happened to e-mail Marc Andreessen, a 22-year-old software whiz who developed the Mosaic Web browser. Together, they founded Netscape — and thus began the Internet revolution.

Orville Wright (1871–1948)/ Wilbur Wright (1867–1912)

The Wright brothers, both of whom had high school education but never received their diplomas, made the first flight on 17 December 1903 in a "flying machine". They later developed the world's first practical airplane and achieved many other aviation milestones.

Their interest in flight was sparked by a toy "helicopter", which their father had bought. They played with it until it broke, then built their own.

In his late teens, Wilbur was struck in the head by a hockey stick in an accident. He became withdrawn and spent the next few years at home caring for his sick mother. He did not attend Yale University as planned, but read extensively in his father's library.

Wilbur later joined the printing business that Orville had started, but seemed to have no particular ambitions. They then opened a bicycle repair, design and manufacturing company in 1892, and they used the workshop for their flight experiments.

Winston Churchill (1874–1965)

Churchill, the British Prime Minister during World War II, is widely regarded as the country's greatest Prime Minister of all time.

As a young boy, he sat for the entrance examination for Harrow School, a public school in London. When he took the Latin paper, a young Churchill carefully wrote the title, his name, and the number 1 followed by a dot — and nothing else!

Despite this, he was accepted at Harrow but placed at the bottom division. He generally did badly and was often punished for poor work and lack of effort. He failed some courses several times and refused to study the classics — Latin and Ancient Greek. But he excelled in English and also sometimes topped his class in History and Mathematics.

Churchill attended the Royal Military Academy Sandhurst and joined the army at age 20. In 1899, at age 25, he entered politics but failed to get elected, and subsequently worked as a newspaper war correspondent.

Churchill was elected to Parliament in 1900 and became Prime Minister only 40 years later, during World War II. Britain had lost confidence in the way Neville Chamberlain, who was then Prime Minister, was handling the war. On 10 May 1940, Chamberlain resigned.

Chamberlain wanted a successor who would command the support of all three major parties in the House of Commons. After meeting with the other two party leaders, he asked Churchill to be Prime Minister and form an all-party government.

Two lesser-known facts about Churchill are worth highlighting: (1) he became Prime Minister again from 1951 to 1955; and (2) he also won the Nobel Prize for Literature in 1953 for his many books on English and world history.

Wernher von Braun (1912–1977)

Von Braun, regarded as the father of the United States space programme, never did well in Physics and Mathematics — until he was inspired by a book, *Die Rakete zu den*

Planetenräumen (*The Rocket into Interplanetary Space*) by rocket pioneer Hermann Oberth. From then on, he applied himself fully in order to understand the two subjects and eventually obtained a PhD in Physics.

One anecdote tells of a 12-year-old von Braun being inspired by the Chinese legend of Wan Hu, "the world's first astronaut". According to legend, early in the 16th century, Wan Hu decided to launch himself into outer space using China's advanced rocket and fireworks technology. He had a chair built with 47 rockets attached. On the day of lift-off, Wan Hu climbed into his rocket chair and 47 servants lit the fuses and ran for cover. There was a huge explosion. When the smoke cleared, Wan Hu and the chair were gone!

After reading this legend, von Braun fired off a toy wagon to which he had attached a number of firecrackers. He was taken into custody by the local police until his father came to collect him.

Von Braun led Germany's rocket development programme before and during World War II. Towards the end of the war, he migrated to the US where he worked on the American Intercontinental Ballistic Missile (ICBM) programme. He then joined the National Aeronautics and Space Administration (NASA), where he served as Director.

Walt Disney (1901–1966)

Walt Disney, the creator of Disneyland and Mickey Mouse, spent most of his childhood days playing on a farm. His father's ill health led to the family selling their farm and moving to the city. There, they purchased a newspaper route and Disney and his brother had to wake up at 3 a.m. every morning to deliver newspapers.

Disney began attending grammar school in 1910, and later enrolled in classes at the Kansas City Art Institute. Because of his early-morning newspaper runs, he often fell asleep in class and was prone to daydreaming and doodling.

In high school, Disney was the cartoonist for the school newspaper, *The Village Voice.* He also began taking night courses at the Chicago Art Institute.

Disney dropped out of high school at age 16 to join the US Army, but was too young to enlist. Later, he tried to join the American Red Cross and the St John's Ambulance, and finally got in by forging his birth certificate, changing his birth date from 1901 to 1900.

Ray Croc, the founder of MacDonald's, was a buddy of Disney in the army. He once commented:

> *"Whenever we had time off and went on the town to chase girls, he stayed in the camp drawing pictures."*

Pablo Picasso (1881–1973)

Picasso is not only one of the best known modern artists, but also the most prolific — with about 13,500 paintings, 100,000 prints and engravings, 34,000 book illustrations and 300 sculptures. Given that many of the prints and ceramics were released in an average of 75 editions, the total number of original Picasso works is over a quarter of a million.

Picasso's father was an art teacher and he attended mostly art schools where his father taught. He never finished his college-level course of study at the *Academia de San Fernando* (Academy of Arts) in Madrid, leaving after less than a year.

As an interesting side-note, Picasso also suffered from dyslexia, a learning disorder which causes difficulty with reading and writing.

Gamal Abdel Nasser (1918–1970)

Nasser, President of Egypt from 1956 to 1970 and considered one of the greatest Arab leaders in history, failed six times during his first nine years of schooling. The reason for this? Politics.

Nasser became interested — and actively involved — in politics when he was only 11 years old, and attended his first political demonstration while still a schoolboy. During his last year of secondary school, he reportedly spent only 45 days actually in school. In 1935–1936, he was chairman of a committee of Cairo secondary school students interested in Egyptian political reform.

In 1937, he joined the Egyptian Military Academy and, for a while, abandoned his political activities. After World War II, he worked to organise reform-minded military officers and in 1949, the group adopted the name Free Officers. On 23 July 1952, Nasser and the Free Officers launched a coup and installed General Muhammad Naguib as President and Prime Minister.

A conflict between Naguib and Nasser led to Naguib's resignation on 23 February 1954. Nasser was subsequently proclaimed Prime Minister. However, popular demonstrations forced him to hold free elections. Naguib won the elections and reassumed the Presidency, after which Nasser resigned.

During his brief time as Prime Minister, however, Nasser had purged pro-Naguib elements in the army. Finally, in October 1954, Nasser removed Naguib from power and established himself as the effective military dictator of Egypt. In 1956, he became President.

Nasser made a "colossal blunder" in 1967 by provoking the Six Days War with Israel. This crisis led to his resignation, but Nasser was later recalled to power by massive public protests in the streets. He continued to serve as President until his death in 1970.

Milton Snavely Hershey (1857–1945)

Hershey founded the Hershey Chocolate Company (today called The Hershey Company), the largest chocolate company in the world.

As a young boy, Hershey attended several one-room schoolhouses, but stopped formal schooling before the fifth grade when his father made him an apprentice in the printing trade.

He left shortly after to work as an apprentice confectioner in Lancaster and, before he was 20 years old, established his own candy business. Later, he learnt the art of making fine caramel and set up the Lancaster Caramel Company.

Hershey attended the 1893 World Fair in Chicago. Impressed by a German-made chocolate-making machine, he bought it immediately and, in 1894, created the Hershey Chocolate Company.

In 1900, he sold the caramel business for $1 million. With that money, he purchased 1,200 acres of land, with an abundant supply of fresh milk from nearby farms, to mass-produce milk chocolate.

As the company prospered, he developed a company town. Today, the town of Hershey prides itself as "the sweetest place on earth".

Hans Christian Andersen (1805–1875)

Hans Christian Andersen, the Danish writer and poet famous for his fairy tales, grew up in poverty. His father was a sickly shoemaker and his mother, an alcoholic. The entire family lived and slept in a single tiny room.

Andersen displayed great intelligence and imagination as a young boy. However, his father died when he was 11 and the young Andersen had to start earning a living. He worked as an apprentice weaver and a tailor, and later in a cigarette factory.

At 14, with his young soprano voice, Andersen became an actor in the Royal Danish Theatre. His career ended when his voice broke, and a colleague referred him to a poet. Andersen then began to write.

A chance meeting with King Frederick VI of Denmark was to change his life. The King took an interest in Andersen and sent him to grammar school.

Andersen was said to have been a backward and unwilling pupil, possibly with a learning disability. He was much older and the odd man out among his fellow students. He later stated that his schooling years were the darkest and most bitter parts of his life.

Before he went to school, however, Andersen had already published his first story, *The Ghost at Palnatoke's Grave*, in 1822.

Frank Lloyd Wright (1867–1957)

Wright, one of the most famous and influential architects of the early 20th century, spent a great deal of his childhood playing with educational blocks developed by Friedrich Fröbel, a German educator who coined the word "kindergarten". Popularly known as Fröbel blocks, they had a great influence on Wright's approach to architectural design.

In 1885, at age 18, Wright attended the University of Wisconsin School for Engineering. But he left in 1887 without taking a degree. While at university, he worked as an apprentice to a builder and professor of civil engineering, and later at an architectural firm.

Wright is best known for practicising "organic architecture", a term he coined. This is a philosophy of architecture which promotes harmony between human habitation and the natural world, so that buildings, furnishings and surroundings become part of a unified, inter-related composition.

In 1955, the University of Winconsin granted Wright an Honorary Doctorate in Fine Arts.

Dhirubhai Ambani (1932–2002)

Ambani built, from scratch, India's largest privately-controlled corporate empire, the Reliance Group. He was the son of a poorly-paid village schoolteacher and, at 16, he stopped schooling after the 10th grade to join his elder brother in Aden, Yemen.

Ambani worked there as a gas-station attendant and later as a clerk in an oil company. Ten years later, he returned to India and started Reliance with a capital of Rs15,000 (US$375).

Over time, the business grew and diversified. Reliance now has interests in petrochemicals, telecommunications, information technology, energy, power, retail, textiles, infrastructure services, capital markets and logistics.

Reliance is the first privately-owned Indian company to make the Fortune 500 list. At the time of Ambani's death in 2002, Reliance had an annual turnover of US$12.3 billion and an 85,000-strong workforce. The company has 4 million shareholders, and it holds its annual shareholders' meeting in a Bombay football stadium.

A poll conducted by *The Times* of India in 2000 named Ambani "the greatest creator of wealth in the century".

Li Ka Shing (1928–)

Li, a Hong Kong entrepreneur said to be the richest man of Chinese descent, was the son of a primary school head. Yet, he had little opportunity for education. Li stopped schooling in 1940 when Japan invaded China, and his family fled to Hong Kong. He was then 12 years old. At 15, his father died of tuberculosis and Li had to support himself and his family.

In Hong Kong, Li's first job was selling watches at his uncle's store. His hard work made him the best salesman at age 17, and general manager at age 19. He then left to join another company to sell metal wares. He was said to have been so successful that his sales commission was seven times that of the second best salesman.

When he was 21, Li opened a factory to produce plastic flowers, and he soon became the largest supplier of plastic flowers in Asia. In 1958, when his landlord raised the rent, Li decided to develop his own property. Thus began his venture into real estate.

Today, his real estate company, Cheung Kong, is the biggest landowner in Hong Kong, responsible for developing one out of every 12 households. The various Cheung Kong companies account for more than 11 percent of the Hong Kong Stock Exchange.

In Hong Kong, it is said that out of every dollar spent, five cents go to Li's coffers. He controls property, banking, construction, plastics, cellular phones, satellite television, cement production, retail (pharmacies and supermarkets), hotels, domestic transportation (sky train), airports, electric power, steel production, ports and shipping.

Hutchison Whampoa, another of Li's companies, controls 12 percent of all container port capacity in the world, including ports in Hong Kong, China, Rotterdam, Panama and Bahamas. It is also the world's largest retailer of health and beauty products, including the A S Watson group, with over 6,800 stores.

Li is ranked by *Forbes Magazine* as the 10th richest man in the world and the richest man of Chinese descent. In 2006, Li became the first recipient of the Malcolm S. Forbes Lifetime Achievement Award for his entrepreneurship and business success. To his fellow residents of Hong Kong, Li is "Superman".

Konosuke Matsushita (1894–1989)

Matsushita, founder of Matsushita Electric (one of the world's largest manufacturers of electrical and electronic goods), not only grew up poor and had limited education, but he actually decided not to study — and he never regretted it.

At age 9, he had to leave his family to work in another city. A chance to study arose when Matsushita was 11 years old. His sister had found work as a clerk in the postal savings bureau and the bureau advertised for an office boy.

His sister and mother thought he should apply for the job, as it provided an opportunity for education. But his father told him:

> *"You should continue your apprenticeship because, in time, you can start your own business and become independent. I believe this is the best option for you; don't change course mid-stream.*
>
> *I know many people who cannot even write their own letters, but they are good businessmen and they can afford to hire people to do such tasks. If you succeed in business, you can employ people to make up for the skills you lack. Don't throw yourself in an office boy job that has no future."*

Looking back, Matsushita saw that his father was right. He said:

> *"Had I quit my apprenticeship and become an office boy, I might not have become what I am today."*

When he was in his early 20s, Matsushita started his business with the equivalent of US$50, went to the verge of bankruptcy, and eventually grew it to having assets worth

US$42 billion at the time of his death. His personal wealth was a staggering US$3 billion.

Despite his limited education, Matsushita also became highly respected as a management guru and philosopher. In 1979, he established the Matsushita Institute of Government and Management, an educational institution whose innovative approach has been described as avant-garde. The Japanese regard Matsushita as "the god of management".

Thomas Edison (1847–1931)

Edison is hailed as the greatest inventor of all time, with 1,093 patents awarded in his name, including the light bulb and the entire system for generating and distributing electricity. He is credited with "inventing" the Modern Age.

Edison is regarded as a genius. Yet some medical experts speculate that he might have been plagued by serious learning difficulties because, in spite of his brilliant mind, he was strangely weak in areas such as cognition, speech and grammar.

In school, Edison displayed symptoms of what is nowadays called Attention Deficit Hyperactivity Disorder, or ADHD. His teachers frequently lost patience with him and, noting that Edison had an exceptionally broad forehead, concluded that his brain must have been "scrambled". His mother, however, was convinced that his large forehead was a sign of superior intelligence. Whether Edison was intelligent or mentally handicapped, he was always thinking differently from other people. He was always "thinking out of the box".

Edison was largely taught at home by his mother. He read history, literature, general science and chemistry, and was fond of poetry. At one stage, a young Edison even planned to read every book on his father's bookshelf, and his parents had to direct him to be more selective.

From young, he was always experimenting. He set up his laboratory in the basement of his home, but his mother soon complained about the strong smell of chemicals and the dangers they posed.

At that time, Edison had started working on a train — he sold newspapers, snacks and candy and had other children sell fruits and vegetables. At 14, he published his own newspaper, the first ever to be typeset, printed and sold on a train.

So he moved his chemicals to a train cabin. During one bumpy journey, some phosphorus dropped on the floor and ignited. The angry conductor hit Edison on the head, aggravating his hearing loss sustained from scarlet fever. Yet, being deaf did not stop Edison from later producing one of the greatest inventions related to sound — the phonograph.

In 1869, Edison was working as a telegrapher with Western Union and he was about to be fired for spending too much time on his experiments. At age 22, he resigned to become a full-time inventor. By 29, he had more than a hundred patents to his name.

In 1879, after hundreds of experiments, Edison produced a light bulb that could last 13 hours. He eventually improved it until it could last over a hundred hours. On 4 September 1882, Edison opened the world's first commercial electric power station for electric lighting, at Pearl Street, New York — the Modern Age dawned.

Jimmy Lai Chee Ying (1948–)

Lai founded one of East Asia's most successful clothing chains, Giordano, as well as two of Hong Kong's and Taiwan's most widely-read publications, *Next Magazine* and *Apple Daily* newspaper.

Born in China, Lai grew up in poverty and dropped out of school after the fifth grade. He was, in his own words, "just selling things on the street, stealing things."

Despite his lack of formal education, Lai is a voracious reader and a self-taught intellectual who names the Austrian free-market economist, Friedrich von Hayek, as his intellectual mentor.

Lai first made his fortune through Giordano, a retailer of affordable clothing widely seen as Hong Kong's version of Gap, Inc. The company he founded in 1981, but no longer owns, today has over 1,500 stores in 31 countries.

Outraged by the 1989 Tiananmen Square massacre in Beijing, Lai decided to launch a magazine that would give a voice to Hong Kong's hopes and fears at a critical juncture in its history.

The magazine, *Next,* made its debut in 1990. It has been described as "brash and controversial", but was an instant success. So was Lai's *Apple Daily* newspaper, which carried both racy and academic articles. At its launch in 1995, 200,000 copies of *Apple Daily* were sold within hours. Lai has since repeated the same success with Taiwan editions of *Next* and *Apple Daily.*

Agatha Christie (1890–1976)

Christie, by far the bestselling English fiction writer of all time, received no formal education. She was taught at home by her mother, who encouraged her to write from an early age. At 16, she learnt singing and piano at school in Paris. She was an accomplished pianist, but stage fright and shyness prevented her from pursuing a career in music.

In a writing career that spanned 56 years, Christie wrote more than 80 books, most of which were detective mystery novels, earning her the title, "Queen of Crime". She is conservatively estimated to have sold more than two billion copies of her books in the English language, plus another one billion in translations in 103 languages. Only the Bible and the works of William Shakespeare have sold more copies.

A stage play by Christie, *The Mousetrap,* holds the record for the longest run ever in London. It opened in November 1952, and as of 2006, is still running after more than 20,000 performances.

In 1971, she was named Dame Commander of the British Empire.

Celine Dion (1968–)

Celine Dion is one of the bestselling female pop artists of all time, best known for "My Heart Will Go On", the theme from the movie, *Titanic.*

Dion grew up as the youngest in a poverty-stricken family of 14 children. She had little or no education, but her family was musically talented and, at age 5, she began singing in a small piano bar owned by her parents.

At 12, she recorded her first song in French. Her brother sent a copy of the recording to a music manager, René Angélil. Angélil was brought to tears by Dion's voice. He decided to make her a star and even mortgaged his home to fund her first record, "La Voix Du Bon Dieu". Dion became an instant star, and Angélil later became her husband.

At 18, Dion watched Michael Jackson perform and she wanted to be like him. Angélil felt that in order for her to be marketed worldwide, she needed to change her image. Dion was sent to school to improve her English, where she learnt the language in three months.

Besides numerous Academy and Grammy awards, Dion won the Chopard Diamond award in 2004, which is presented to artists who have sold over 100 million albums. Dion had in fact sold 175 million albums! As of 2005, only three artists have earned the Chopard Diamond.

Arthur Henderson (1863–1935)

Henderson is the British union leader who co-founded the Labour Party. He won the Nobel Peace Prize in 1934.

Henderson's father, a manual worker, died when he was 9 years old , leaving the family in poverty. He left school to work in a photographer's shop, and later returned to school for another three years when his mother remarried.

At 12, Henderson stopped schooling completely. He first worked at a locomotive factory and, at 17, at a foundry. The dinner hour in the foundry, with its lively discussions, became his classroom. The newspapers were his textbooks.

Henderson developed his speaking skills from being a lay preacher and from joining a debating society. This helped launch his political career, which began with him joining the trade unions in 1892.

In 1900, Henderson was one of the 129 trade union and socialist delegates who created the Labour Representation Committee (LRC). In 1906, the LRC changed its name to the Labour Party. As a unionist, Henderson believed that strikes caused more harm than they were worth, and tried to avoid them whenever possible.

Soichiro Honda (1906–1991)

Soichiro Honda, founder of Honda Motors, spent his early childhood helping his father with his bicycle repair business. At 15, he went to Tokyo to find work, and became an apprentice in a garage. At 22, he returned home to set up his own auto repair shop.

Honda had little schooling. But he was known to be technically ingenious. Once, he used a bicycle pedal rubber to forge his family's seal on school reports that showed him to be a poor student.

What Honda had was passion — a passion for racing, which earned him a speed record in 1936 and later also resulted in an accident that left him with broken bones.

His wife persuaded him to stop racing, and he thereafter concentrated on his business. In 1937, Honda started manufacturing piston rings. In 1948, he sold the piston business to Toyota and started producing motorcycles.

Today, Honda produces the world's bestselling motorcycles, as well as scooters, cars and trucks. The company is also the largest engine maker in the world, with over 14 million internal combustion engines built each year.

Leo Tolstoy (1828–1910)

Tolstoy is regarded as one of the greatest novelists of all time, noted for his masterpieces, *War and Peace* and *Anna Karenina.*

Tolstoy studied law and oriental languages at university, but his teachers described him as "both unable and unwilling to learn". He left university without graduating, and spent his time during and after university in pleasure-seeking — with wine, women and gambling.

Apart from his epic novels, Tolstoy was also noted for his ideas on non-violent resistance. He was a major influence on people such as Mahatma Gandhi and Martin Luther King, Jr.

Abraham Lincoln (1809–1865)

Lincoln, who is widely regarded as the greatest American president of all time, was born to illiterate farmers. He received only about 18 months of formal schooling. Instead, he was largely self-educated and studied every book he could borrow, including the Bible, Shakespeare, English history and American history.

As an adult, however, Lincoln taught himself law and was admitted to the bar in 1837, at age 26. He worked as a lawyer for 20 years and became one of the most prominent lawyers in the state. But he was never successful in financial terms. At times, he convinced his clients to settle their cases out of court, thus earning himself nothing. Often, he declined to collect his legal fees from clients who were poor. In fact, until he was elected US President in 1860, Lincoln was largely unsuccessful in his businesses, careers and political pursuits.

As President, Lincoln preserved the unity of the United States of America by leading the government to victory in a Civil War (1860–1864) that had threatened to divide the country. He also ended slavery, granting freedom to some four million African-Americans.

It has been said that no American president faced a greater crisis than Lincoln did during the Civil War, and no American president has accomplished as much.

Noted for his memorable speeches as well, his most famous, and most often quoted, speech is the Gettysburg Address (1863). It was a short, two-minute speech which closed with him speaking of democracy as "*government of the people, by the people, for the people.*"

Lincoln is consistently ranked the greatest American president of all time. Between 1948 and 2005, 11 major polls were taken of historians, political scientists and other scholars. Lincoln was ranked top in five of the surveys, second in another five, and third in one. Lincoln also came out top in two out of three recent public opinion polls, one conducted in 2000 and the other two in 2005.

Most of all, Lincoln is remembered and loved as a man of integrity and sincerity. His most popular nickname is "Honest Abe".

Benjamin Franklin (1706–1790)

Franklin was a scientist, inventor, statesman, civic leader, writer, businessman and more. He was considered one of the greatest minds of the 18th century.

Yet, Franklin had minimal education as he came from a large family. He attended less than a year of grammar school. Although he did well and was promoted to the second year before he had completed the first, he left school before the year was up. He then studied another year in a private school — where he learnt reading and writing but failed Arithmetic — before he stopped schooling completely.

He was, however, very fond of reading. He could read from a very young age and spent all his free time during his youth reading. Whatever money he had, he used it to buy books.

Franklin regularly networked with other intellectuals. At age 21, he established *Junto*, a society of young men who met on Friday evenings for self-improvement, study and socialising. It was from the *Junto* that many of Franklin's ideas and civic projects arose. This included support for the use of printed currency and the establishment of a public library, fire brigade, fire insurance, etc.

In 1743, he established the American Philosophical Society to network with learned people from around the world.

Franklin devoted his entire life to learning and self-improvement. His two final inventions, which came when he was close to 80 years old, were both for the pursuit of knowledge. One was a "long arm" for taking books from high shelves. The other was bifocal lenses to help him read better.

inspire

7

Be Inspired!

There are two possible ways to respond to the stories of Benjamin Franklin, Abraham Lincoln and all the other "famous failures" mentioned in the previous chapter. One way is to think of all the reasons why we cannot seem to succeed like them. Perhaps they lived in a different era, or had other special reasons for their extraordinary success.

Think again. Today, even the average school dropout has six or more years of schooling, much more than many of the "famous failures". Most of us also have free or low-cost access to hundreds of thousands of books in public libraries. With the Internet, our access to knowledge and information is greater than ever before.

The point is not to compare. When we look at others, they will always be better off than us in some ways, worse off in others, and yet similar in many ways.

A more appropriate response to an outstanding success would be to be inspired — inspired to achieve similar levels of success and excellence, with or without education.

There is no secret to this. The "famous failures" achieved their success by having a Prizedream and working hard for it. They lived by their own internal rules, such as being different and taking control of their life situations. They took advantage of opportunities that passed their way, and also created opportunities for themselves.

The "famous failures" possessed many of the qualities of a leader, such as wisdom, sincerity, strictness and benevolence. They devised strategies to turn setbacks into advantages. They worked hard for success until it became their habit and part of their character, and achieved cycle after cycle of success unlimited.

These are not extraordinary measures. They are ordinary things that you and I can do. There is a PRAISE Champion in each and every one of us, just as there was one in each of the "famous failures". What they did was merely to nourish that PRAISE Champion and allow it to emerge and manifest itself in their lives. Many people have done it, and so can you.

This is not to say that it will be easy. Just as there is a PRAISE Champion inside us, there is also a "robber" inside us who would deny us our potential for success and greatness. It is not easy to remove this robber, as the robber may be very deeply entrenched.

Like many people, I was once ruled by this robber. I was very, very far from achieving success and excellence. But because I had a strong desire to excel, I slowly climbed out of my failure and misery. I changed my environment and, instead of being surrounded by equal failures, I began to surround myself with friends who were able to help me, and genuine in wanting to do so.

I do not believe in making false promises and telling you that just because you have read this book, you can, overnight, become an extraordinary success. Perhaps some of you can. But for most of us, it is going to take some time.

But you can make a start — by aiming for small successes.

PRAISE will help you escape mediocrity and conformity to lead yourself to accomplish your own unique vision by unlocking your hidden potential.

PRAISE has helped me achieve excellence and success in the past 20 years and counting, in different facets of my life — studies, examinations, career and entrepreneurship. It also helped me overcome other life's challenges, such as when I climbed Mount Sinai, the "Mountain of Moses". More recently, PRAISE enabled me to embark on a new adventure to become a writer and publisher.

I may not be a "famous failure", but I am certainly one "failure" who succeeded in life. My wish is to inspire you to draw out the PRAISE champion that dwells inside you, and that you might inspire others to do the same.

Let us inspire one another!

PRAISE is simple, yet powerful.

Use it or miss it. The choice is yours.

Think. Reflect. Engage.

The Self

Influenced by SADDLE

- ***S***elf-pity
- ***A***rrogance
- ***D***aydreams
- ***D***istractions
- ***L***aziness
- ***E***xaggerated fear

Adopts PRAISE

- ***P***rizedream
- ***R***ules
- ***A***nalysis
- ***I***nvincibility
- ***S***trategy
- ***E***xcellence

Acquires six SUCCESS formulas

- Change
- Creativity

- Passion
- Fulfilment
- Learning
- Excellence

For a lifetime!

PRAISE Model

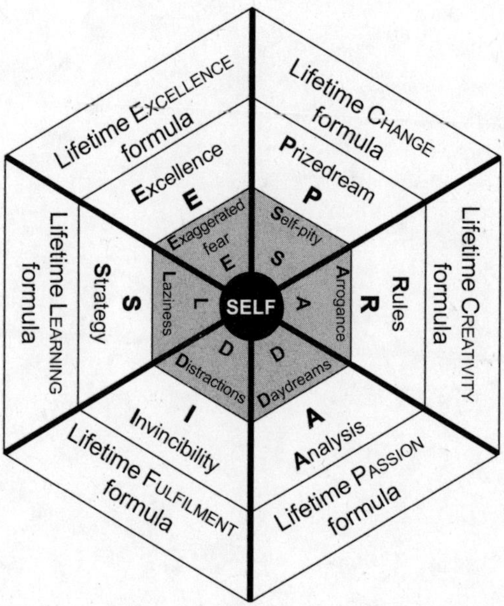

Six lifetime SUCCESS formula

inspire

8

Sixteen Soulprints

(Excerpts from *Soulprints I — BreakThrough*)

1. Endurance

My mother put me down, went to the doorway and came back carrying her pair of slippers. I never noticed them before. They were worn out with holes. For the first time too, I saw the soles of her feet — rough, ugly soles, too ugly for a lady. "It is all about endurance," my mother said.

2. Self-reliance

It occurred to me that I had obtained the slippers through my own means. I felt very proud of myself. Earlier, I was thinking that the trishaw boy knew how to make money. I realised that I had done the same — I had sold my champion spider for $2.

3. **Self-acceptance**

I felt great respect for the one-legged man who endured the difficulty of moving about with crutches. Even though he did not talk much with anyone, he did not look very sad either. He seemed to have accepted his fate. It was all about accepting oneself.

4. **Resilience**

My mother had to learn to swallow her tears. Her daughter had run away. Her twin sons had dashed her hopes. But she had to learn to bear with the pain and get up every time she was hit, as the family still needed her. It was all about resilience.

5. **Determination**

I continued to squat on the beach and watch the waves come and go. As one wave subsided, the next wave came. They never gave up. They seemed to be telling me never to give up too.

6. **Perseverance**

The tear-jerking reunion between mother and Phoenix left a deep imprint in my memory. Seeing how my mother's persistent efforts paid off in changing Phoenix's attitude affected me in a deep way even as a child. It taught me to have faith in persevering.

7. **Trustworthiness**

   I finally understood where my mother had obtained her money from. She must have managed to borrow from friends and relatives. They trusted her because she was a lady of her word. It was all about trustworthiness.

8. **Love**

   She was determined that I should not lose my arm. She wanted me to be able to lead a normal life. She wanted all this for me when nobody else in the family cared as much, or simply did not care at all. Love propels one to action. Love conquers all.

9. **Self-discipline**

   That thin, underweight and undernourished primary school boy had now become the "Strong Boy". I was proud of my transformation. It made me realise that, with self-discipline, it was possible to change myself for the better.

10. **Humility**

    If there was anything I had learnt from my experience with my tutor, Victor, it was humility. One should always maintain humility whether one has achieved success or encountered a setback. With humility, one can improve and move on in life.

11. Helpfulness

I told the class about Hwa's plight and urged my classmates, as well as my friends from the other classes, to donate whatever money they could. Helping a person from the heart produced such a wonderful feeling. It was all about helpfulness.

12. Backbone

She feared that if I took up Rachael's loans, I would be indebted to her for life. My mother thus made her position very clear. If I wanted to go overseas for my studies, I must rely on my own means to do so. It was all about backbone.

13. Steadfastness

My mother also believed that, eventually, things would turn out well. Her marriage to my father took a very long time to improve, but already, my father had become a changed man.

14. Vigilance

She always had to be on the lookout for surprise raids, since her bread stall was unlicensed. At first, she would cut her fingers because she had to be vigilant and cut bread at the same time. Likewise for my two sisters. But after a while, they got used to it.

15. Invincibility

My mother said she had failed so many times in her lifetime. But she always bounced back. As much as she wanted me to succeed, my mother wanted me to be able to bounce back from failure. It's all about not being defeated by failure.

16. Modesty

My mother advised me to be modest about my achievements. When her bread stall became profitable, she did not like to boast about how much she earned. Because of my mother's modesty, some customers would rather queue up to buy bread from her.

My Soulprints 心之旅

Endurance 忍耐

Self-reliance 自立

Self-acceptance 自纳

Resilience 弹力

Determination 决心

Perseverance 毅力

Trustworthiness 诚信

Love 爱心

Self-discipline 自律

Humility 虚心

Helpfulness 热心

Backbone 骨气

Steadfastness 坚定

Vigilance 警惕

Invincibility 常胜

Modesty 朴实

定风波

莫听穿林打叶声，何妨吟啸且徐行。
竹杖芒鞋轻胜马，谁怕？一蓑烟雨任平生。
料峭春风吹酒醒，微冷，山头斜照却相迎。
回首向来萧瑟处，归去。也无风雨也无晴。

苏东坡 (1037–1101)

I hear the wind and the rain beating against the
leaves; but I continue to play my flute and
move on through the trees.

A bamboo walking stick and a pair of straw shoes
make a journey lighter than riding on a horse;
what's there to fear when a straw hat takes me
through the wind and rain throughout
my journey in life.

A gust of wind in the spring wakes me up; the wind
is a little cold but the oblique rays from the
mountains warm me up.

I look back at the tumultuous road which I had
just travelled; they are all gone: the wind, the
rain and the sun.

— Su Dong Po (1037–1101)

inspire

Thank You

for reading this book.
We hope you have enjoyed it.
We shall be happy to receive your feedback
and be of further service to you.
Please contact us at:

Endorsements for
Soulprints I — BreakThrough

BreakThrough *was particularly moving because of your graphic, brutally honest description of your early life in Singapore. I could not put the book down until I completed the last page.*

– Dr Vivian Balakrishnan, Singapore Minister for Community Development, Youth and Sports

Very engaging and well-written... sounds a bit like a male version of Wild Swans... *a compelling story.*

– Catherine De Vrye, Australian Executive Woman of the Year and bestselling author of *Good Service is Good Business*

This is a wonderful book of courage, perseverance and inspiration that can take your life to new heights.

– Brian Tracy, motivational speaker and bestselling author of *Million Dollar Habits*

This book has equal horror and hope. It reminds me of a cross between Angela's Ashes *and a treatise on the redemption power in all of us — a triumph of human spirit.*

– James Clemins, bestselling author of *Shadow Fall: Book One of 'The God Slayer Chronicles'*

Endorsements for
Benjamin Franklin — A Bright Spark!

Clearly, there will be many conferences, books, exhibitions... planned for the Franklin 300th. However, there may not be a tribute as valuable as Benjamin Franklin — A Bright Spark!

– Roy E. Goodman, Curator of Printed Materials, American Philosophical Society, Pennsylvania and President, Friends of Franklin, Inc

In all of my years studying Franklin... I have never found a book as important as this. Every person should read it. Every parent should make sure their children read it.

– Ralph Archbold, the official 'living Benjamin Franklin', member of US Federal Commission appointed by President George W. Bush and Congress to oversee the celebrations of Benjamin Franklin's 300th birthday

George Tan capsulises, in this 'must-read' book, the heart and soul of lifetime success, and then he backs it up with a real-world model for implementing that success you won't easily forget.

– Anne Bruce, life coach, professional speaker and best-selling author of *Discover True North: A 4-Week Approach to Ignite Your Passion and Activate Your Potential*

No ordinary biography but a brilliantly researched and exceptional read. Buy it, read it and you will also recommend it.

– Richard Denny, top motivational speaker and bestselling author of *Succeed for Yourself*

Endorsements for
Rough Life Rich Life

Rough Life Rich Life *is a rich book — rich in information, rich in wisdom, rich in experiences and, most significantly, rich in inspiration.*

– Dr Tony Alessandra, bestselling author of *The Platinum Rule,* exclusive Speaker Hall of Fame and one of top 20 motivational speakers in the world

Dream what you want to dream, go where you want to go, be what you want to be ... George Tan dared to dream. He overcame extreme poverty and parental abuse. The life skills model that he presents is an invaluable guide to those who strive for excellence in spite of the challenges they face.

– Michael McGrath, Executive Director and Co-founder of The Muscle Help Foundation

George Tan, speaking of his Prizedream, is an inspiration to many. I find him to be sincere, passionate, and realistic with his challenges.

– Edward Horrell, bestselling author of *More Than Words*

Endorsements for
Red Marks to Flying Colours

Red Marks to Flying Colours *is more than just a book about how to achieve success in school. Author George Tan shares his personal experiences of overcoming tremendous setbacks in transforming himself from being a gangster kid who failed English and Mathematics, to a top student and a successful entrepreneur. This book is both instructional and inspirational.*

– Willie Jolley, bestselling author of *It Only Takes a Minute to Change Your Life* and *A Setback is a Setup for a Comeback!*

Within a few short pages of George Tan's latest book, I was hooked and could not put it down. George presents a life skills model for success in studies and beyond, weaving in his engaging story of how he made that quantum leap from Red Marks to Flying Colours. If you need inspiration, this is a must-read.

– Rev Dr John L. Clements, international speaker and success coach, author of *Fruitful Prospects* and *Excellence Becomes YOU*

Flying Colours *is a book that will inspire and educate, and you will enjoy reading it from beginning to end. George's ideas and concepts will motivate anyone to want to be better at their career and their life!*

– Hal Becker, bestselling author of *Lip Service*

Endorsements for
Scholars' Secrets: How to Get Your A's

Scholars' Secrets *is a practical, insightful and engaging work that spurs readers to transform their goals and dreams into reality.*

– Ang Wee Hiong, CEO/Principal of Hwa Chong Institution

George Tan has painstakingly charted the reasons why many fail in examinations and do not perform to expectations. More importantly, he provides a clear and proven path for these apparent 'low performers' to achieve high results and get out of their 'failure streak'.

– Dr Kirpal Singh, academic, writer, critic and educationalist

Students will find this book opens their minds to possibilities for personal growth, scholastic achievement and self-fulfilment.

– Vicki de Prazer, Australian Olympic Team psychologist 1996, 2000, 2004

inspire